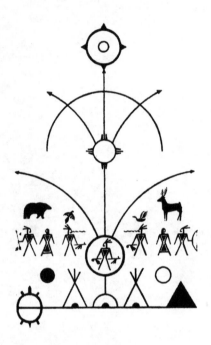

This Ojibway logo by Del Ashkewe from Cape Croker symbolizes the content of the book. The large circle at the top with four projections represents Kitche Manitou, the Creator. A circle symbolizes spirit; to denote Great Spirit, a larger circle was circumscribed around a smaller. The four projections indicate universal presence.

The inverted semi-circle below the symbol for Kitche Manitou represents sky and universe. Immediately below is the symbol of the Sun; it represents life and time, linear and cyclic.

Under the Sun is the image of man within a sphere. Together they represent human life and existence and being.

Conjoining the symbol for life to the symbol for Kitche Manitou is the line of life and power: with the two branches on either side sweeping upward and outward denoting the Tree of Life, plantkind upon which all beings are sustained.

The base for the Life-line and the Tree of Life formed by a straight line represents the earth and rock, the substance of Mother Earth. The teepees in different styles image tribes, communities, societies and families and mean different styles and modes of living.

On either side of the figure of the encircled man are other men and women. Those nearest to the central image with wavy lines emanating from their lips reflect speech, history, languages and stories. Next to the speakers are women, symbols of the primacy and constancy of womankind. The figures most remote from the centre mirror sustenance and patterns of life. The four orders of animals, Tree of Life, earth, and men and women represent being, and existence and time.

OJIBWAY HERITAGE

BASIL JOHNSTON

University of Nebraska Press
Lincoln and London

First Bison Book printing: 1990

Library of Congress Cataloging-in-Publication Data
Johnston, Basil.
Ojibway heritage / Basil Johnston.
p. cm.
Reprint, with new preface. Originally published: Toronto: McClelland
and Stewart, c1976.
ISBN 0-8032-7572-2
1. Ojibwa Indians—Religion and mythology. 2. Ojibwa Indians
—Legends. I. Title.
E99.C6J64   1990
299'.783—dc20
89-24959 CIP

Reprinted by arrangement with McClelland and Stewart

∞

Contents

Turtle, *reproduced by permission of Del Ashkewe.*

Preface to the Bison Book Edition

In the fall of 1969, Dr. E. S. Rogers, curator-in-charge of the Department of Ethnology of the Royal Ontario Museum in Toronto, invited me to serve on a search committee that had been struck and entrusted with the task of selecting a candidate who was to develop an "Indian" program. At the end of three months there was not a single application for the position of "lecturer." Alarmed that the grant that had been extended by the federal government for the position might be withdrawn and forever lost, Dr. Rogers and the committee asked if I would accept the position on an interim basis until a candidate was found.

I started as a "fill-in" on January 1, 1970, by teaching in the Ethnology Galleries and working out a plan for the development of an "Indian" program. No candidate having applied for the position by the end of June, Dr. Rogers asked me to remain for another year.

During that summer we decided that, as part of the program come September, I should visit schools around Toronto and the Native communities in southern Ontario. For the next two years I went from school to school delivering talks with the use of artifacts from the collections as teaching aids.

Within a short time I grew weary of holding up objects and describing their use, naming the several parts and explaining how and where they were acquired; the students seemed equally disinterested in the ethnographic aspects of old moccasins. On intuition I began to combine stories that bore tribal insight with ethnography, even though I was uncertain what it was that students wanted to know or what it was they didn't want to know.

My uncertainty continued until 1973. That winter I was invited to attend, as a special guest, an Indian display assembled by the grade-five students of Churchill Avenue Public School in North York as a grand finale to their six-week in-depth study of Indians. Students, teachers and parents were justifiably proud of the exhibition.

1

The entire library was one large gallery. Against the walls were tables bearing pictures, sketches, maps, books, charts drawn by the students, scrapbooks, and artifacts, such as arrowheads, quill boxes, shards, baskets, and figurines on loan from private collections. On the walls were posters, maps, calendars and several large pictures of warriors and chiefs. At one end of the library was a large canvas teepee with a tripod of poles in front to represent an outdoor fireplace. Their faces painted with rouge, mascara, eyeshade and lipstick, students wearing homemade costumes and either paper headdresses or real seagull, crow, or partridge feathers atop their heads mingled with the visitors. They acted as guides and answered questions about their respective tribes, whose names were printed on cardboard badges: ALGONQUIN, IROQUOIS, SIOUX, HURON, OJIBWAY but no FOGRIB, KUTCHIN or SLAVEY.

In front of the teepee stood a grim-looking chief, his arms folded. Like the rest of the Indians his face was painted in hostile, warlike colours. I went directly to him.

"How!" I said in greeting.

The Blackfoot chief examined me quizzically.

"How come you look so unhappy chief?"

"Sir! I'm bored," the chief replied.

"How so, chief?"

"Sir! Don't tell anybody but I'm bored. I'm tired of Indians. That's all we've studied for six weeks. I thought they'd be interesting when we started because I always thought that Indians were neat. At the start of the course we had to choose to do a special project from food preparation, transportation, clothing and some other topics. I chose dwellings," and here the chief exhaled in exasperation, "and that's all me and my team studied for six weeks, sir! Teepees, wigwams, longhouses, igloos. We read books, encyclopedias, went to the library to do research, looked at pictures, and drew pictures. Then we had to make one. Sir! I'm bored."

"Didn't you learn anything else about Indians, chief?"

"No sir! There was nothing else . . . Sir? . . . Is that all there is to Indians?"

As best I could in the short time that I had with him, I tried to assure that bored young student that there was more, much more than presented in books.

His question ("Is that all there is to Indians?") made a powerful impression on me that has remained ever since and I'm indebted to him for his candor. Because of his remark, I began to examine and to evaluate what books about Indians were available to him, as well as other students and their teachers. From that moment I reassessed how I should go about developing an "Indian" program within the Department, the Museum, and the community at large.

Saying that he was bored because Indians were boring was, as I saw it, another way of saying that the course that he and his colleagues had just endured was shallow, without the substance that they had anticipated or deserved. That grade-five student and others like him wanted to know more than how Indians organized themselves, how they fished and hunted, how they cooked, what they ate, what they wore, how they moved from one place to the next in summer or winter, or how they fought. They thirsted intellectually.

Students such as this fifth-grade youngster are as interested as are adults in other people, other races. They are often more tolerant and receptive than adults to cultural differences. They want to know what other children of other races do and what they are required to learn; they want to know what other races think about matters more important than dwellings; they want further to know how other races feel in order to enrich their own understandings and broaden their outlooks.

Students want to know in what respect others are different from or similar to themselves, whether those others are selfish or unselfish, honest or deceitful, bold or cautious, imaginative or dull. They want to touch the mind and heart of that Indian chief whose face shows no trace of emotion; they want to be touched by the mind and the heart of that woman who carries on her back a papoose bound in a cradle-board as she bends over her work. They wonder if these Indians, these savages, these children of nature laughed or cried, feared nothing, or ever trembled in fright. Whether nine-, ten-, eleven- and twelve-year-old boys and girls fully understand what they study of others is debatable and doesn't matter, they still want to know and ought to be given the opportunity.

Besides being open to new ideas, youngsters are more ready to learn than adults believe because of their sensitivity. They are more interested in the hunter than in bows and arrows, more in the grandmother than in the shirts that she is sewing. Once I realized this trait about the young, I never again adverted to the origin, purpose, antiquity of the tribal craftsman who made the

3

weapon that I had on display. Instead, I told stories in which the artifact in hand had but a minor role.

Few stories move the sensitivities of young students as much as does "The Man, the Snake and the Fox." In it the bow and arrow, the knife, and the clothing of the man are next to irrelevant.

In its abbreviated form the story is as follows. The hunter left his lodge and his family at daybreak to go in search of game in order to feed his wife and his children. As he proceeded through the forest, the hunter saw deer, but each time they were out of range of his weapon.

Late in the afternoon, discouraged and weary, he heard faint cries in the distance. Forgetting his low spirits and fatigue, he set out with renewed optimism and vigor in the direction of the cries. Yet the nearer the hunter drew to the source of the cries, the more daunted he was by the dreadful screams. Only the thought of his family's needs drove him forward; otherwise he might have turned away.

At last he came to a glade. The screams and shrieks and groans came from a thicket on the opposite side. The hunter, bow and arrow drawn and ready, made his way forward cautiously.

To the hunter's horror, in the thicket was an immense serpent, tangled fast in the vines as a fish is caught in the webbing of a net. The monster writhed and roared and twisted as he struggled to break free.

The man recoiled in horror but before he could back away, the snake saw him.

"Friend!" the snake addressed the man.

The moment that the snake spoke, the man fell in a heap on the ground. When he came to much later the snake pleaded with the man to set him free. For some time the man refused but he eventually relented, persuaded by the monster's plea that he too, though a serpent, had no less right to life than did the man. But it was the serpent's promise that he would not do injury to the man on his release that convinced the hunter.

But the moment that the last vine was cut away the snake sprang on his deliverer.

The uproar created by the man and the snake in their struggles attracted a little fox who happened to be in the vicinity. Never having seen such a spectacle, the fox settled down to watch. Almost at once it was evident that the man was about to be killed.

Curious to learn why the snake and the man were in mortal

4

struggle the little fox interrupted the mayhem by shouting and asking for an explanation.

After the man gasped out his story, the snake gave his version. By pretending not to understand the snake's explanation the fox beguiled the aggressor into returning to the thicket to show by demonstration what he meant.

In the demonstration the snake entangled himself once more.

When he saw that he had been delivered from the edge of death by the fox, the man was so moved that he felt bound to show his gratitude in some tangible way. And, even though the fox assured him that there was no need for the man to make requittal, the hunter nevertheless persisted in pressing his deliverer to tell him how he, the hunter, might perform some favor on behalf of the fox.

Not only was there no need, the fox explained, there was as well nothing that the man could do for the fox; there was not a thing that the fox needed or desired of human beings. However, if it would make him happier, the fox suggested that the man might feed him should he ever have need.

Nothing would please the man more than to perform some good for his deliverer; it was the least that he could do for a friend who had done so much.

Some years later the hunter shot a little fox who had been helping himself to the family storage. As the man drew his knife to finish off the thief, the little fox gasped, "Don't you remember?"

That no snakes as monstrous as the one in the story are to be found on this continent makes no different to the youngster's sense of outrage over the treachery of the snake and the forgetfulness of the man; nor does the exercise of speech that enables the snake and the fox to communicate with the hunter and each other prevent the young from being moved to compassion for the fox. Their sense of justice and fairness bears them over the anomalies in the story.

Before the last words "Don't you remember?" have echoed away, the young begin to ask questions. "Why? Why did that man not recognize the fox? Why did he forget? How did the man feel afterwards? Why did the snake attack the man? Why did the snake break his promise? Why didn't the man leave the snake where he was? Do animals really really have as much right to live as human beings do?"

Only after the young have raised these questions about the

more important issues concerning human nature and conduct, timeless and universal, do they focus on the more immediate particulars. "How do Indians know whom to trust? What did they do when someone deceived them? Does one good turn really deserve another? What's the range of an arrow? How did the Indians prepare their food for storage? How long would it keep? How much would they have to put away? Suppose they didn't put enough away, what then?" And many other questions were generated by this story.

It was precisely to inspire such questions and to implant in the minds of youngsters the idea that Indians, like other races, had interests and cares about matters other than bodily needs that I told audiences my tribe's stories. Even if youngsters of nine, ten, eleven, and twelve are not ready to resolve the questions they had in mind, they at least begin to think about them.

Regrettably, giving talks reaches only a small audience and in the nature of things they are likely to be soon forgotten.

Beyond the confines of Toronto and the Indian reservations of Southern Ontario was a much larger audience, larger than could ever be reached by the spoken word. The only way that wider audience could be reached was through publication.

There was also another reason for considering writing. The development of a program or a guideline or a curriculum and the successful implementation of that program depends on the availability of good texts. In my opinion, the books on Indians then in circulation were not good enough.

Presumptuous as was the idea of writing a text that would supplant the ones currently in print, I nevertheless made the decision to do so. Two other matters, level and content, had to be resolved before the work could begin. Reaching the widest possible audience my object, I decided to write for adults and teachers who would then pass on to children what they had read. Content was not so easily resolved until I asked myself what it was that my tribe and my people would like other people to know about our culture.

With this in mind I planned to write booklets in imitation of those by Dr. E. S. Rogers, popularly known as the Rogers series. But the texts were so uneven in length that they did not readily lend themselves to booklet form, whose format is set in multiples of four. Out of this dilemma was born a book, *Ojibway Heritage*.

Preface

If the Native Peoples and their heritage are to be understood, it is their beliefs, insights, concepts, ideals, values, attitudes, and codes that must be studied. And there is, I submit, no better way of gaining that understanding than by examining native ceremonies, rituals, songs, dances, prayers, and stories. For it is in ceremony, ritual, song, dance, and prayer that the sum total of what people believe about life, being, existence, and relationships are symbolically expressed and articulated; as it is in story, fable, legend, and myth that fundamental understandings, insights, and attitudes toward life and human conduct, character, and quality in their diverse forms are embodied and passed on.

But it is not enough to listen to or to read or to understand the truths contained in stories; according to the elders the truths must be lived out and become part of the being of a person. The search for truth and wisdom ought to lead to fulfilment of man and woman.

It is in the hope that the heritage of the Ojibway speaking peoples and their Algonkian brothers and sisters will be a little better understood that this book was written, though it represents but a small portion of the total fund of unwritten tradition. It is one way of perpetuating and enhancing the bequest of our forefathers as it is a means of sharing that gift with those whose culture and heritage may be very different but who wish to enlarge their understanding.

What is difficult in an undertaking of this kind is retaining the substance of the meaning of the stories while changing the images, metaphors, and figures of speech which must necessarily be done during any translation and interpretation from one language to another — in this instance, from

7

Ojibway into English. Readers are asked to bear in mind that like any other language, Ojibway makes liberal and imaginative use of images, metaphors, and figures of speech to express in the concrete abstract ideas and concepts. The stories recorded are not to be interpreted literally; but freely, yet rationally according to the Ojibway views of life. Readers and listeners are expected to draw their own inferences, conclusions, and meanings according to their intellectual capacities.

Because each Ojibway story may embody several themes and meanings, time and deliberation are required for adequate appreciation. There is no instantaneous understanding. Ojibway stories are as broad and deep in meaning and mystery as are the tales, legends, and myths of Greek, Roman, Egyptian and other peoples and just as difficult to understand as are the parables in the Bible.

Fortunately Ojibway stories are flexible in nature and scope. It is for this reason that they are best narrated. Skill and imagination will enable the story-teller to impart any level of meaning according to the scope and ability of his audience.

Many, if not most of the stories, related in this book will be found to be similar to the stories of the Cree, Abenaki, Blackfoot, Micmac, Menominee, and other Algonkian speaking peoples. That this is so ought not to be astonishing. The similarities that exist simply suggest a common view of life.

For the stories that I have recorded I am indebted to innumerable story-tellers in Ontario; for the understandings, I gratefully acknowledge the guidance of Edward Kaghee (deceased); Aylmer Plain; Gregor Keeshig; Tom Medicine; Maria Seymour; Fred Greene; Jane Rivers; Flora Tabobandung; Fred Wheatley; William Meawassige; Mike Trudeau (deceased); Rose McLeod (deceased), my grandmother; Sam Zawamik; for allowing me scope and for their encouragement, thanks to Dr. E. S. Rogers and Dr. H. Fuchs, my colleagues in the Department of Ethnology; for support, to the woman I love and my family; for typing, to Margaret Cozry; for patience and latitude to my employer, the Royal Ontario Museum; and to Anna Porter for considering my manuscript worthy of publication.

I would like to state that I have not received any benefit from any patron, fund, foundation, or council in the preparation and writing of this book.

OJIBWAY HERITAGE

Moose, *reproduced by permission of Norval Morrisseau.*

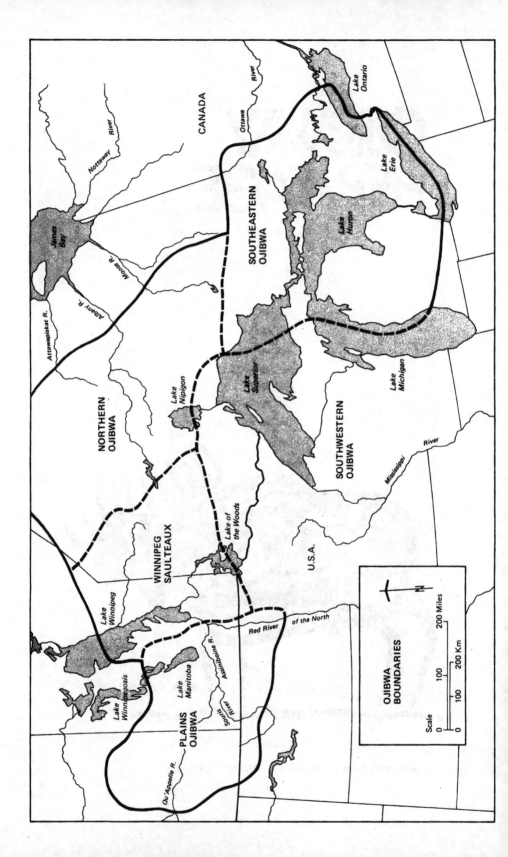

The Vision of Kitche Manitou

CREATION

Young and old asked:
 Who gave to me
 The breath of Life
 My frame of flesh?
 Who gave to me
 The beat of heart
 My vision to behold
 Who?

 When to Rose the gift
 Of shade, of beauty
 And grace of form?
 When to Pine the gift
 Of mystery of growth
 The power to heal
 When?

 How to Bear the gift
 Of sense of time
 A place of wintering?
 How to Eagle came the gift
 Of glance of love
 The flash of rage?
 How?

 Who gave to Sun
 His light to burn
 His path to tread?
 Who gave to Earth

Her greening bounty
Cycles of her being?
Who?

Who gave to us
The gifts we do not own
But borrow and pass on?
Who made us one?
Who set the Path of Souls?
Who carved the Land of Peace?
Who?

As the young asked, the old men and old women thought about these matters.

They gave their answers and explanations in the form of stories, songs, prayers, rituals, and ceremonies.

Kitche Manitou (The Great Spirit) beheld a vision. In this dream he saw a vast sky filled with stars, sun, moon, and earth. He saw an earth made of mountains and valleys, islands and lakes, plains and forests. He saw trees and flowers, grasses and vegetables. He saw walking, flying, swimming, and crawling beings. He witnessed the birth, growth, and the end of things. At the same time he saw other things live on. Amidst change there was constancy. Kitche Manitou heard songs, wailings, stories. He touched wind and rain. He felt love and hate, fear and courage, joy and sadness. Kitche Manitou meditated to understand his vision. In his wisdom Kitche Manitou understood that his vision had to be fulfilled. Kitche Manitou was to bring into being and existence what he had seen, heard, and felt.

Out of nothing he made rock, water, fire, and wind. Into each one he breathed the breath of life. On each he bestowed with his breath a different essence and nature. Each substance had its own power which became its soul-spirit.

From these four substances Kitche Manitou created the physical world of sun, stars, moon, and earth.

To the sun Kitche Manitou gave the powers of light and heat. To the earth he gave growth and healing; to waters purity and renewal; to the wind music and the breath of life itself.

On earth Kitche Manitou formed mountains, valleys, plains, islands, lakes, bays, and rivers. Everything was in its place; everything was beautiful.

Then Kitche Manitou made the plant beings. These were four kinds: flowers, grasses, trees, and vegetables. To each he gave a spirit of life, growth, healing, and beauty. Each he placed where it would be the most beneficial, and lend to earth the greatest beauty and harmony and order.

After plants, Kitche Manitou created animal beings conferring on each special powers and natures. There were two-leggeds, four-leggeds, wingeds, and swimmers.

Last of all he made man. Though last in the order of creation, least in the order of dependence, and weakest in bodily powers, man had the greatest gift — the power to dream.

Kitche Manitou then made The Great Laws of Nature for the well being and harmony of all things and all creatures. The Great Laws governed the place and movement of sun, moon, earth and stars; governed the powers of wind, water, fire, and rock; governed the rhythm and continuity of life, birth, growth, and decay. All things lived and worked by these laws.

Kitche Manitou had brought into existence his vision.

DESTRUCTION

Disaster fell upon the world. Great clouds formed in the sky and spilled water upon the earth, until the mountain tops were covered. All that was left was one vast sea. All men died. All the land creatures perished. All the plants were covered by the sea. Only the water animals and birds and fishes lived on. What was once earth was a huge unbroken stretch of water whipped into foam and wave by the ferocious winds.

The world remained a sea for many generations.

RE-CREATION

At length the rains ceased, the clouds vanished, and the sun shone.

High in the heavens there lived alone a woman, a spirit. Without a companion she grew despondent. In her solitude she asked Kitche Manitou for some means to dispel her loneliness. Taking compassion on the sky-woman, Kitche Manitou sent a spirit to become her consort.

Sky-woman and her companion were happy together. In time the spirit woman conceived. Before she gave birth her consort left. Alone she bore two children, one pure spirit, and the other pure physical being.

The new beings of opposite natures and substances hated one another. In a fiery sky battle they fought and destroyed each other.

After the destruction of her children, the spirit woman again lived in solitude. Kitche Manitou knowing her desolation once more sent her a companion. Again sky-woman conceived. As before her consort left but sky-woman remained content.

The water creatures observed what was happening in the heavens, sensed the weariness of the spirit woman, and pitied her. In their compassion, they sought ways to provide relief for her. Eventually they persuaded a giant turtle to rise to the surface of the waters and offer his back as a haven. When the great turtle agreed, the water beings invited the sky-woman to come down.

The sky-woman accepted the invitation, left her abode in the skies, and came down to rest on the back of the great turtle. When sky-woman had settled on the turtle, she asked the water animals to get some soil from the bottom of the sea.

Gladly all the animals tried to serve the spirit woman. The beaver was one of the first to plunge into the depths. He soon surfaced, out of breath and without the precious soil. The fisher tried, but he too failed. The marten went down, came up empty handed, reporting that the water was too deep. The loon tried. Although he remained out of sight for a long time, he too emerged, gasping for air. He said that it was too dark. All tried to fulfil the spirit woman's request. All failed. All were ashamed.

Finally, the least of the water creatures, the muskrat, volunteered to dive. At his announcement, the other creatures laughed in scorn, because they doubted this little creature's strength and endurance. Had not they, who were strong and able, been unable to grasp soil from the bottom of the sea? How could he, a muskrat, the most humble among them, succeed when they could not?

Nevertheless, the little muskrat determined to dive. Undaunted he disappeared into the waves. The onlookers smiled. They waited for the muskrat to emerge as empty handed as they had done. Time passed. Smiles turned into worried frowns. The small hope that each had nurtured for the success of the muskrat turned into despair. When the waiting creatures had given up, the muskrat floated to the surface more dead than alive, but he clutched in his paws a small morsel of soil. Where the great had failed, the small succeeded.

While the muskrat was tended and restored to health, the spirit woman painted the rim of the turtle's back with the small amount of soil that had been brought to her. She breathed upon it and into it the breath of life. Immediately the soil grew, covered the turtle's back, and formed an island. The turtle had given his service, which was no longer required and he swam away. The island formed in this way was called Mishee Mackinakong, the place of the Great Turtle's back, now known as Michilimackinac.

For his service to mankind and the spirit woman, the turtle became the messenger of thought and feeling that flows and flashes between beings of different natures and orders. He became a symbol of thought given and received. The turtle, slowest of all creatures, represented celerity and communication between beings.

The island home grew in size. As the waters subsided, the animal beings brought grasses, flowers, trees, and food-bearing plants to the sky-woman. Into each she infused her life-giving breath and they lived once more. In the same way were the animals who had drowned revived. Everything was restored on that island home.

At last the time came for the sky-woman to fulfil the promise of life. One cloudless morning she gave birth to twins, a boy and a girl.

The new beings were unlike her first children who had destroyed one another. They were composite in nature, made up of physical substance and a soul-spirit substance. In this respect they were similar, yet at the same time they encompassed vast differences. One was a man; the other was woman. Although they were different, they tended toward union with one another. Neither was complete or fulfilled without the other. Only together did they possess meaning; only together could they fulfil their purposes.

What was unique was the soul-spirit of each. Called "cheejauk" it was made up of six aspects: character, personality, soul, spirit, heart or feeling, and a life principle. This substance had the capacity to dream and to receive vision. Through dream and vision a man would find guidance in attaining fulfilment of self.

For men the vision was necessary for self-fulfilment; for women a vision was not essential. By giving life through the first mother, women were fulfilled. Just as Kitche Manitou had received a vision and brought it to fulfilment, so had men to quest for it and live it out once they received it.

Men and women had yet another aspect. Each possessed his "chibowmun," or aura. It was a substance emanating from his "cheejauk," through his body by which the state and quality of his inner being was sensed and felt.

The new men and women were called "Anishnabeg," beings made out of nothing, because their substances were not rock, or fire, or water, or wind. They were "spontaneous beings."

The cycle was complete, creation, destruction, and re-creation.

In the first year, the animal beings nourished and nurtured

the infants and the spirit woman. For all their needs the spirit woman and her children depended upon the care and goodwill of the animals. The bears, wolves, foxes, deer, and beaver brought food and drink; the squirrels, weasels, racoons, and cats offered toys and games; the robins, sparrows, chickadees, and loons sang and danced in the air; the butterflies, bees, and dragonflies made the children smile. All the animal beings served in some tangible way; all except the lowly dog.

Of the animal beings, the dog was endowed with the least exceptional powers. He was less fleet than the fox; he was weaker than the wolf; he was less cunning than the mink. Compared to the fisher, the dog was a poor swimmer; beside the deer, the dog was awkward. Less gifted than his brothers, the dog had nothing to offer. He could not serve. Nevertheless he felt constrained to do something. In his despondency, he pledged to give his love. Others could serve according to their natures and capacities; he to his.

Consequently, the dog settled down by the side of the bed in which the sleeping infants lay, alternately sitting or lying down. He gazed into their eyes, placed his head near their feet, or played to amuse them. The babies smiled. From that time on the dog never left the side of man.

The first winter in the life of the Anishnabeg was an ordeal. Food was scarce; the winds were harsh. The infants grew sick and lost strength daily. It seemed that they would not survive the winter. The spirit woman was disconsolate, and the animals and birds were alarmed that the babies they had grown to love would die. The bear, fearing the death of the infants, offered himself that they might live.

With the bear's sweet flesh, the infants survived. The death of the bear encompassed life for the new beings. Thereafter, the other animals sacrificed their lives for the good of men. When the infants grew into manhood and womanhood, they bore a special love for the bear and honoured him in their ceremonies. In gratitude and fondness they dedicated a prayer to the other animals, "I had need." Men and women survive and live because of the death of their elder brothers.

Many years later when the first Anishnabeg had grown up and spirit woman was certain of their survival, she called her children to her. She told them that she was returning to the Land of Peace, to her proper place of abode. She also told them that when they had lived out their term of life and had done sufficient good in life, they too would leave their bodies in the Land of the Living and go to the Land of Peace as soul-spirits, and live there in another way.

16

Then the spirit woman ascended into the sky to return to her home. Thereafter the Anishnabeg remembered the first of Mothers, Nokomis (Grandmother) whenever the moon gave light. At the same time, they remembered the primacy of women, who bore the unique gift of life, for it was through woman that the cycle — creation, destruction, re-creation — was completed. For her special gift of giving life and being, women had a special place in the order of existence and were exempt from the vision quest.

After the spirit woman returned to her own realm, the Anishnabeg prospered and increased in numbers. Animals and men and women laboured readily and happily together. Michilimackinac was a happy home to all.

This happy state did not last. A strange and fatal disease afflicted the Anishnabeg and threatened to wipe them out. For this dread disease there was no medicine; from this affliction, no relief or escape was possible. Many died. Fear and sadness prevailed among those who had not yet become ill.

One of the victims of this plague was a young boy, Odaemin. After a short illness he died, leaving his father, mother, brothers, and sisters. At death his soul-spirit travelled westward for four days along the Path of Souls before coming to a fog enshrouded ridge. At the entrance to the Land of Souls the boy interceded for life for his people. Restored to life, he related the conditions for admittance into the Land of Souls and delivered the promise made by Kitche Manitou that an intermediary, who would teach the Anishnabeg what was essential for their existence and well being would be sent.

In the meantime they had to await the coming of the teacher before their miserable condition could improve.

Kitche Manitou sent Nanabush to teach the Anishnabeg.

NANABUSH KITCHE MANITOU'S EMISSARY

Nanabush was born of a human mother, sired by a spirit, Epingishmook, (The West). Like his older brothers, Mudjeek-awis, Papeekawis, and Chibiabos, Nanabush possessed supernatural powers and was a spirit in nature.

By the time that Nanabush was born, his older brothers had left home. He knew them only by name. Not long after his birth Nanabush's mother died, although some said she had been destroyed. Nor did Nanabush know his father. Without parents Nanabush was raised and nurtured by his grandmother.

During his early years, Nanabush was like any other boy. He had much to learn. What learning and wisdom he acquired came from his grandmother.

As he grew older, he often questioned his grandmother about his origin and about his father and his mother. Nanabush did not get any explanation. "Later," said Nokomis. "When you are older," she promised.

By the time he grew into manhood, Nanabush came to realize that he possessed powers not possessed by others. It was at this point that his grandmother told him about his mother and her death. She also disclosed to Nanabush that his father was still alive and living in the west.

Angry, Nanabush set out to find his father and avenge his mother. He decided to test his own powers and those of his father in spite of his grandmother's objections. Nanabush made his way westward toward the Land of the Great Mountains, carrying only his bow and arrows and a small medicine bundle which an old man had given him.

At last, after many months, he came to mountainous country. Tired, and not certain how to find or recognize his father when he met him, Nanabush encamped under a great tree.

As he sat, pondering how he might find and meet his father, Nanabush heard someone call his name.

"Nanabush, beware of Epingishmook. He has great powers. He knows that you are here, and he means to come to destroy you. Go to the place of flint. Gather the pieces. Collect them and put them into a bag. Sharpen them; give them another force. They, in turn, will give you another power. They have within them the element of fire. Carry them with you always. Use flint. It is the only substance your father fears. It will injure him, but it cannot destroy him."

Nanabush looked up into the tree and saw only a woodpecker chipping away at the tree. Nanabush knew that it was woodpecker who had delivered the warning and given the advice. Grateful, he thanked the bird.

Immediately Nanabush went to the place of flint, gathered as many fragments as he could carry, and bundled them up. On his return to camp Nanabush sharpened the pieces.

While Nanabush was busy sharpening and polishing the flint, his father arrived. Nanabush greeted his father with respect but, at the same time, with fear and suspicion. Nanabush's father was massive, and appeared still young and unafraid.

Together they talked all afternoon and far into the night. When the east was beginning to show the dawn, Nanabush told his father the purpose of his journey. "Father, I have come to avenge my mother's death. I have come to punish you for killing my mother, whereby I have been denied a mother's love."

18

Epingishmook looked at his son sadly and warned him, 'My son, you may harm me, but you cannot destroy me. Neither my injury nor my death will restore your mother or allow you to know a mother's love. You are more spirit than man. Beware, your own powers are limited and may betray you."

Nanabush, though fearful, was not cowed. Rising up, he answered, "What you say may be true, but tomorrow I will fight you."

The next day, as agreed, Nanabush met his father on the great plain. The battle began. Epingishmook fired arrows that sizzled like bees; Nanabush hurled flints that whistled. All day the battle raged, with no advantage gained on either side. The missiles darkened the sky like clouds. That evening, the contestants, having exhausted their arrows and flints, (although Nanabush, mindful of woodpecker's warning kept one small piece tied around his neck with a thong), met in hand-to-hand combat. Such was the violence of the fight that great clouds of dust rose into the skies and the earth trembled. When it seemed that the fight was going against him, Nanabush took out the flint he had concealed and slashed his father's head with it, cutting him deeply. As soon as the blood began to flow, Epingishmook conceded. Nanabush ceased fighting.

Epingishmook addressed his son, "My son, you have great powers. You are my equal, not more, not less. For all your powers you cannot vanquish me, nor I, you. Let us make peace. I shall remain in my place. Return to the Land of the Anishnabeg. Teach them until they are strong. In this way you and your purpose will be fulfilled and you will know love. As a remembrance of our contest and peace, take this pipe; carry it with you always. It is the emblem of peace and goodwill. Give it to the Anishnabeg."

Nanabush took the pipe and thanked his father. Together they smoked the Pipe of Peace, and composed their hearts and minds. After smoking, Nanabush returned to the Great Lakes to serve the Anishnabeg and to carry out his purpose.

Nanabush had much to learn about the nature, extent, and limitations of his powers. Not only had he to learn what they were, he had to develop them, and foster their growth.

Nanabush was a supernatural being. As such he possessed supernatural powers. Of all the powers he possessed, none was more singular than his power of transformation. As a tadpole changes into a new being with a new form, as a caterpillar becomes a butterfly of dazzling beauty, so could Nanabush assume at will, and in an instant, a new form, shape, and existence. Nanabush could be a man, and change to a pebble in the next instant. He could be a puff of wind, a cloud fragment, a flower, a toad. And though Nanabush could become a physical being, essentially he was a supernatural being.

It was the only way that Nanabush could accomplish his purpose. As pure incorporeal being he would be neither accepted, nor understood. He learned this early in his association with the Anishnabeg. Beings accept and understand only their own kind. A man understands and accepts another man, an eagle, another eagle. Whatever form or shape he assumed, Nanabush had also to accept and endure the limitations of that form and nature.

If he were to become an eagle, Nanabush could soar among the clouds, but he could not swim or dive as a duck. He could become a pine, stately and enduring, but then, he could not sing or run. A pine he was in form and nature. Were he to become a man or woman, he could be as courageous or fearful as a man or woman could be; he could be generous or miserly; he could be true or he could be false; loving or hating. As an Anishnabe, Nanabush was human, noble and strong, or ignoble and weak.

For his attributes, strong and weak, the Anishnabeg came to love and understand Nanabush. They saw in him, themselves. In his conduct was reflected the character of men and women, young and old. From Nanabush, although he was a paradox, physical and spirit being, doing good and unable to attain it, the Anishnabeg learned. For his teachings, they honoured Nanabush.

Father Sun and Mother Earth

After Nanabush and his father, Epingishmook, had fought, they smoked the Pipe of Peace as a symbol of reconciliation, goodwill, and harmony between them.

Epingishmook explained the ritual that he performed: "The Anishnabeg are to remember as they smoke their special relationship to and dependence upon the sun, earth, moon, and stars. Like the animal beings they depend ultimately upon the earth and the sun.

"There are four orders in creation. First is the physical world; second, the plant world; third, the animal; last, the human world. All four parts are so intertwined that they make up life and one whole existence. With less than the four orders, life and being are incomplete and unintelligible. No one portion is self-sufficient or complete, rather each derives its meaning from and fulfils its function and purpose within the context of the whole creation.

"From last to first, each order must abide by the laws that govern the universe and the world. Man is constrained by this law to live by and learn from the animals and the plants, as the animals are dependent upon plants which draw their sustenance and existence from the earth and the sun. All of them depend ultimately on the physical world. The place, sphere, and existence of each order is predetermined by great physical laws for harmony. It is only by the relationships of the four orders that the world has sense and meaning. Without animals and plants man would have no meaning; nor would he have much more meaning if he were not governed by some immutable law. For the well being of all there must be harmony in the world to be obtained by the observance of this law.

"While there is a natural predilection and instinct for conformity to the great law of balance in the world of plants and animals, mankind is not so endowed by nature. But man possesses understanding by which he can know and abide by the law and so establish his place in the world order. Man must seek guidance outside himself. Before he can abide by the law, mankind must understand the framework of the ordinances. In this way, man will honour the order as was intended by Kitche Manitou."

> The sun has his own path
> Gives and withdraws his light
> The earth
> Responds abundantly.

FATHER SUN

From the earliest times the Anishnabeg honoured the physical world of the sun, moon, earth and stars; of thunders, lightnings, rains, winds, mountains, and fires.

Superseding all was the sun. Even the position of the lodges reflected reverence for the sun. The entrance to the lodge faced the east or, as it was known, "The Dawn." By custom the first person rising from sleep, "half-death," went out, faced the east, thought and uttered a prayer.

> By you, Father
> Through the sun
> You work your powers
> To dispel the night
> Bring day anew
> A new life, a new time.

> To you, Father
> Through the sun
> We give thanks
> For your light
> For your warmth
> That gives light to all.

A further connection between the sun and man was deduced from the daily experience of dawn and dusk — the annual regeneration and dissolution of life. Each morning as the sun rises, the flowers open, the birds begin to warble, the animals begin to stir, and the shadows fade away. The sun infuses life into all things. And each evening with the set of the sun, the roses enfold themselves, the robins become silent, the animals go to sleep. When the sun withdraws light, he also reduces life. In the spring when the sun grows warm, the whole world regenerates; in autumn, when the sun is less warm, life

22

departs leaving only shadows of what was, and shades of what will be. In lifegiving, the sun is the father of all.

Just as the Anishnabeg rendered prayers of thanks in the morning, so did they give thanks in the evening for the gifts received during the day.

But the analogy of sun and man-father goes beyond the obvious and the physical to symbolize the relationship of the begotten to God or Kitche Manitou. The sun served only to symbolize this relationship and this theological understanding.

Prayers of thanksgiving were part of daily life and living, not separate from man's labour or recreation, nor cribbed in ritual. As the giver gave freely and generously, so the receiver must acknowledge his gratitude in the same spirit. To the Anishnabeg there was no gift or giving without a recipient. At the same time the recipient must know how and in what terms to acknowledge benefits. The gift of life is given once, but it is renewed daily in each dawning.

There is yet another aspect to the gifts bestowed by Kitche Manitou. Everyone shares in the gifts of light, life, and warmth. Thus no one person may presume that the gift is intended for him alone or deny the enjoyment of such gifts to another. All have received, all must acknowledge the great bounty.

MOTHER EARTH

The Anishnabeg predicated fatherhood of the sun. In the same way they proclaimed motherhood in the earth. Both sun and earth were mutually necessary and interdependent in the generation of life. But of the two pristine elements, Mother Earth was the most immediate and cherished and honoured.

In function both Father Sun and Mother Earth were different, just as man and woman are dissimilar. The sun illumnates, the earth sustains with beauty and nourishment. One cannot give or uphold life without the other.

Perhaps motherhood of Earth emanated from its elemental substance, rock. As such, it seemed to remain unchanged, enduring winds, winter and summer. It appeared immune to change that man could see immediately, unmoving as it were, so as to live on in order to give life. The same kind of character and quality was expected of motherhood whose foundation was love. If children were to grow into manhood and womanhood, they had to have confidence in the abiding nature of the love of motherhood, otherwise they would be wanting in trust in themselves and in others. But the constancy of the earth in life giving and in the bounty of her giving was more assumed than that of human motherhood.

To Father Sun was given reverence, to the earth the Anishnabeg gave love and honour. They prayed.

Woman!
Mother!
From your breast
You fed me.
With your arms
You held me.
To you, my love.

Earth!
Mother!
From your bosom
I draw nourishment
In your mantle
I seek shelter
To you, reverence.

Just as the Anishnabeg saw the sun as a symbol of the fatherhood of man, so they saw in the earth, motherhood. A woman, by a singular act with a man conceives and gives birth to new life. Thereafter she must sustain the new life.

In a similar way the earth responds. With the coming of spring and the warmth of the sun, the earth conceives and gives birth to flowers, grasses, trees, and food-bearing plants. She then nourishes them. As a woman deserves honour and love for her gift of life, so does the earth deserve veneration.

In honouring the earth through prayer, chant, dance, and ceremony the Anishnabeg were honouring all motherhood in a special way.

The love and respect that the Anishnabeg felt for the earth was perpetuated in the Pipe of Peace Smoking Ceremony. The first whiff of smoke was offered to Kitche Manitou; the second to Mother Earth. It was an integral part of the ceremony without which the ceremony would have been incomplete and, therefore, void. Such was the way in which the Anishnabeg publicly demonstrated their dependence on the earth and veneration for the primacy of womanhood.

Nor did the veneration for the earth end with the breath of smoke. There was yet another tangible way in which the motherhood of earth was venerated. In the Pipe of Peace Smoking Ceremony the four orders of life and being were represented: earth, plant, animal, and man. The earth, whose elemental substance was rock, made up the pipe; the plant, tobacco, was the sacrificial victim; the animal, symbolized by feathers and fur, was appended to the sacred pipe of rock; man was the celebrant.

The rock was strong and enduring. Plant beings, animal beings, and man come to an end, but the earth lives on. Mother Earth continues to be be bountiful, sustaining all beings. All else changes; earth remains unchanging and continues to give life. It is a promise to the future, to those yet to be born.

There is in addition to constancy in Mother Earth, generosity. This attribute is acknowleged in prayer and ceremony.

A mother begets a child. She nourishes him, holds him in her arms. She gives him a place upon her blanket near her bosom. A woman may give birth to many children. To all she gives food, care, and a place near her. To each she gives a portion of herself; to each she assigns a place in the household. No child by virtue of priority of birth or other attributes may demand for himself more than his brothers or sisters. A mother gives equally to all of her children, from first to last, from strong to weak. All are entitled to a place near her bosom in her lodge. Her gift does not diminish but increases and renews itself.

Similarly is the earth bounteous. Her mantle is wide, her bowl ever full and constantly replenished. On the blanket of Mother Earth there is a place for hunting, fishing, sleeping, and living. From the bowl comes food and drink for every person. All, young and old, strong and weak, well and ill are intended to share in Mother Earth's bounty and magnanimity.

The principle of equal entitlement precludes private ownership. No man can own his mother. This principle extends even into the future. The unborn are entitled to the largesse of the earth, no less than the living. During his life a man is but a trustee of his portion of the land and must pass on to his children what he inherited from his mother. At death, the dying leave behind the mantle that they occupied, take nothing with them but a memory and a place for others still to come. Such is the legacy of man: to come, to live, and to go; to receive in order to pass on. No man can possess his mother; no man can own the earth.

Men and ages linger, and then pass on. Mother Earth remains whole, indivisible, and enduring. With death ends ownership and possession. Men do not outlive the earth; earth outlasts man.

As beneficiaries of their mother's care and love, children are obliged to look after their mother in her illness and decrepitude.

Men and women owe their lives and the quality of living and existence to Mother Earth. As dutiful and loving children, they are to honour Mother Earth. The most suitable and fitting way of expressing this affection is by rendering in song and prayer the feeling of the heart. Because they love her, they avoid harming or injuring the earth. The debt of life must be acknowledged from the heart and mind.

Mother Earth gives life; she takes it back. In pain, sickness, and in sorrow a child turns to his mother for relief and comfort. A man or woman in suffering seeks repose upon the bosom of mother. They do not go to the father but turn to a woman for solace. All beings do this. Plants in dissolution bend before they collapse on the soil. Animal beings stricken by arrow or at last overcome by age lay down upon the ground. Men and women recline upon the earth in the final moments of life. It is then, as in birth, that children are closest to their mothers.

Symbolically then, and in a very real way, men and women give their lives back to Mother Earth. Interred in the bosom of Mother Earth with only their personal possessions, the dead find rest, and in time become part of and one with Mother Earth. At birth a man receives his life from his mother; in death he gives up his life to Mother Earth.

The Anishnabeg loved the Earth, the soul-spirit of which was beauty, growth, bounty, and peace.

GRANDMOTHER MOON

The first of mothers, having given birth to her children, nurtured them to manhood and womanhood. Her purpose and nature fulfilled, she returned to her own world. But before her ascension, she reminded her children that she would not forget them. She would, she assured them, continue to watch over them at night through the moon. For their part, the children promised to remember the first of mothers whenever the moon appeared in the sky.

By day Father Sun and Mother Earth looked after the children; by night Grandmother Moon shone in the heavens to guide men's paths. Thus is the primacy of womanhood remembered.

GRANDFATHER THUNDER

The first father of the Anishnabeg, being a spirit, returned to the heavens after the conception of the twins. Unlike the first mother, who was remembered and honoured, the first father was forgotten. He had not left a token, a sign, or a mark by which he could be remembered.

Animkee (Thunder), for that was his name, became despondent and bitter over the neglect and forgetfulness of his grandchildren. In his anger he emerged from the western skies calling out in a voice that reverberated across the heavens. Obscured in the clouds, he crossed directly over the homes and the villages of the Anishnabeg. In his fury, he shot lightning arrows at the earth, and whipped the clouds until they cried their tears upon the earth. He seldom remained but passed on toward the east.

At first he was alone. Later he was joined by many other grandfathers. Together and numerous they often stormed the Anishnabeg.

Men and women were terrified whenever great clouds formed, lightnings flashed, and thunders shook the skies. From Nanabush the Anishnabeg learned to offer the sacred tobacco to the grandfathers. Thereafter it became the custom to offer tobacco to the Thunders.

To Anishnabeg, the tree, the creature, the portion of earth pierced by a lightning arrow was deemed to possess medicine and power, a special essence.

More distant from the grandchildren than is the grandmother, grandfathers are not to be less remembered and honoured. They too have shared in the gift of life and in guiding the destinies of grandchildren.

WAUSSNODAE (Northern Lights)

In winter the grandfathers remain near their lodges and do not venture abroad. They keep their fires burning. It is the reflection of their fires that is seen in the northern skies, sometimes bright, sometimes faint, sometimes vivid, sometimes soft.

It was also said that the northern lights were the glow of torches that the grandfathers used to illuminate the Path of Souls for the soul-spirits on their way to the Land of Peace.

The Anishnabeg remembered their grandfathers. It was from their ancestors that the Anishnabeg inherited their understandings of life and being, all that they were and ought to be. What the grandfathers left as a legacy was the product of their minds, hearts, and hands. The living were to accept the gift, enlarge it, and then pass it on to the young and the unborn. For the grandfathers there was to be thankfulness and remembrance.

THE FOUR QUARTERS

Kitche Manitou created four incorporeal beings: Zhawano (South), Keewatin (North), Waubun (Morning or East), and

Ningobianong (Evening or West). He assigned each one to a quarter of the world and to a portion of time. To each he gave a power over life to be exercised with wisdom. Legend relates that these beings lived in harmony.

With the coming of the plant and animal beings and the Anishnabeg, the guardian beings tested one another in battle.

This is the way the strife began.

A man and his wife had a daughter who was cheerful, industrious, kind, beautiful, and clever. Such qualities attracted many suitors, who came with their flutes to her village and lodge to woo her. One by one, each was tested for his courage and generosity; each was required to prove his hunting and fishing skills by supporting the family for a period of time. One by one, each was found wanting in some quality essential in caring for a companion in life.

At last a youg man from a distant village arrived. Kind and gentle, he brought flowers and berries to the young girl. Moreover he constantly sang with a voice of great beauty. The girl fell in love with Zeegwun, the young man. Her parents took Zeegwun into their home for testing and found him suitable, well able to care for their beloved daughter. A marriage was arranged for the autumn, when the young couple would sew their garments together as a symbol of their union.

Late that summer another young man from far away came to the village. He had heard of the beauty, cleverness and kindness of the girl, and, although she was promised, loved her at once. A warrior, he was bold, strong and brave, with many feathers in his war bonnet. As a hunter no one was his equal. Soon after his arrival he had challenged and defeated all the young men of the village.

Bebon, for such was his name, went in search of Zeegwun, whom he had not encountered in his contests with the young men of the village. Zeegwun, gentle and mild, was no match for the mighty Bebon, who left him lying battered and bleeding, senseless on the ground.

Day after day, for no apparent cause, Bebon returned to assault the unfortunate Zeegwun. It seemed that Bebon harboured a special hatred for the docile Zeegwun. Upon no other did Bebon vent his rage. With each beating, Zeegwun became weaker, and more broken. The people looked after him in pity. As time went by, the respect of the people for Zeegwun diminished, while the respect for Bebon increased. Bebon laughed when the battered Zeegwun slunk from the village, promising to return.

Bebon, the mighty hunter, remained. Each day he left

early, to return late in the evening with game of all kinds, ducks and partridge, moose, deer, and bear. He showed the women of the village where to find abundant berries and vegetables. With his skill he fed not only the family of his beloved, but the entire village.

In war Bebon was equally capable. Not only was he the foremost warrior in his adopted village, he was the most formidable war leader in the nation. Marauding war parties were repulsed and enemy villages invaded under his leadership, until his name was feared and the village was safe.

Bebon was honoured; Bebon was respected; Zeegwun was forgotten.

But Zeegwun did come back to the village of his betrothed. Stronger and more vigorous, he came seeking vengeance. He met Bebon, who was returning weary and hungry from a long hunting expedition. Zeegwun meeting Bebon, insulted him, slapped his face. Then he attacked Bebon savagely, cut his face, and knocked him unconscious.

Zeegwun waited by the unmoving form of Bebon. As soon as Bebon recovered, Zeegwun again assaulted him. The fight continued day after day until Bebon pleaded for mercy, promising to leave the village and the country.

With Bebon gone, Zeegwun was able to win back the love of the girl, and the respect of her people. Once more there was warmth and beauty in the land.

That autumn Bebon returned, fully recovered from his injuries. In a short time he drove Zeegwun into exile again. When spring came, Zeegwun returned to triumph over Bebon.

So it went, year after year, Bebon and Zeegwun battling for supremacy, fighting for the hand of the maiden, engaging in a contest in which there was no victor, no vanquished.

The girl grew discouraged; her parents tired of the never-ending warfare between Zeegwun and Bebon. In order to bring the feud to an end, and to remove their daughter from the love of two such contestants, the parents placed her on an isolated bay, some distance from the village. Her home floated on the waters so that neither of her suitors could reach her easily. Still the battles did not cease.

When the girl died, unmarried and unfulfilled she was transformed into a water lily, a constant reminder of the folly of seeking love from war. The purity of its petals and fragrance remind everyone that war can harm the innocent harmless creatures that take no part in the conflict.

Even with the death of the maiden, the annual struggle of Zeegwun (Summer) and Bebon (Winter) continued. Zeegwun brought renewal, youth, and life. In victory, Bebon brought dissolution, decay, and death. Neither could establish permanence to their regime.

While Bebon and Zeegwun struggled to win the hand of the maiden they loved, another struggle arose. Waubun (Dawn) and Ningobianong (Star Sinking in Waters or Evening) began their duel.

Both were very powerful medicinemen possessing and controlling vast knowledge and potent medicines. Ningobianong was the elder and the tutor of Waubun.

After many years of study under Ningobianong, Waubun felt that he was ready to conduct his own practice of medicine without the supervision or tutelage of his teacher.

When he approached Ningobianong with a request for independence Ningobianong refused on the grounds that Waubun's knowledge of skills was incomplete.

Waubun, confident and assured, challenged Ningobianong to a demonstration of their powers. Ningobianong agreed. Since he was younger, it was arranged that Waubun was to work his powers first. Many of the early Anishnabeg came to the contest as spectators.

Waubun, young, proud, and strong announced, "I shall stop the sun in the eastern sky so that it will always be morning." As he wished the sun stopped. The Anishnabeg were amazed and glad. For a long time the sun remained unmoving.

Waubun turned to Ningobianong and taunted the old man. "Mighty Ningobianong, can you match that".

Ningobianong turned his gaze toward the sun, and it began to move toward the western hills, became a brilliant crimson ball, and sank out of sight.

Waubun and the assembled Anishnabeg were astonished. Nevertheless Waubun arose to his feet.

"I shall make the sun rise again. With its rising all the flowers shall open their petals to greet his coming."

Just as Waubun willed, so did the sun rise and all the flowers open to greet him.

Ningobianong remained calm. He nodded his head, and the sun transversed the heavens and once more sank out of sight. As the sun disappeared all the flowers once again enfolded themselves.

But Waubun was not discouraged. He said to the crowd, "With the next rising of the sun, I shall take the first born and make him ever youthful."

Next morning a new born baby was brought to Waubun. The medicine man breathed upon the child. The Anishnabeg watched and were glad. The child grew. Still the Anishnabeg watched. They marvelled at the power of Waubun. In their admiration they asked Waubun for the gift of youth.

"Wait," said Ningobianong. "It is my turn."

The Anishnabeg hissed at Ningobianong.

Ningobianong took the young man by the hand and looked into his eyes, said, "You shall lose your youth."

The Anishnabeg watched, and as they watched they saw that it was so. The young man changed. He lost his youth and vigour. The man became feeble, and he became wise.

Amazed and fearful the Anishnabeg withdrew saying that neither medicine man was more powerful than the other. Waubun and Ningobianong continued their contests, disregarding this judgement, day after day, month after month, life after life.

The Nature of Plants

THE TREE OF LIFE

A tree images life
It grows
Unwell, it heals itself
Spent, it dies.

A tree reflects being
It changes
Altered, it restores itself
Ever to remain the same.

A tree gives life
It abides
It lends existence yet
Endures undiminished.

Trees give me everything
Serve all my needs
To the tree I can give nothing
Except my song of praise.

When I look upon a tree
I remember that
The apple tree can
Allay my hunger
The maple can
Slake my thirst
The pine can
Heal my wounds and cuts
The bark of birch can
Form my home, can

Mould my canoe and vessels
The tissue of birch can
Keep the images that I draw
The balsam groves can
Shield me from the winds
Fruit of the grape vine can
Lend colour to my quills
The hickory can
Bend as my bow, while
The cherrywood provides
An arrow shaft.

The cedar ferns can
Cushion my body in sleep
The basswood can
Become my daughters' doll
The ash, as snowshoe, can
Carry me across the snows
The tobacco can
Transport my prayers to God
The sweetgrass can
Aromate my lodge
The roots of evergreen can
Bind my sleigh and craft
The stump and twig can
Warm my lodge
The rose and daisy can
Move the soul of woman
The leaves wind-blown can
Open my spirit.

The elders said that Kitche Manitou created the world in a certain order; first, the physical world of sun, moon, earth and stars; second, the plant world of trees, flowers, grasses, and fruits.

Plants were therefore prior to animals and to the Anishnabeg. They could exist alone; they were not dependent upon other beings for their existence or well being.

In essence each plant being of whatever species was a composite being, possessing an incorporeal substance, its own unique soul-spirit. It was the vitalizing substance that gave to its physical form, growth and self-healing. This inner substance had a further power. It could conjoin with other members of its own species and, more wonderful, with other species to form a corporate spirit.

Each valley or any other earth form — a meadow, a bay,

a grove, a hill — possesses a mood which reflects the state of being of that place. Whatever the mood, happy, peaceful, turbulent, or melancholy, it is the tone of that soul-spirit. As proof, destroy or alter or remove a portion of the plant beings, and the mood and tone of that valley will not be what it was before.

Each plant was given a soul-spirit whose scope was determined by its physical form and substance.

Some Anishnabeg believed that the soul-spirit of a plant was unique, unlike any other; others thought that the soul-spirit of plant was that of being, not admitted into the Land of Souls, but returned to earth to complete its term of being and existence and to attain internal peace.

The legend of Odaemin symbolizes this belief. Odaemin was turned back from the Land of Souls because his soul-spirit was in turmoil. He returned to the Land of the Living to live out this life as a heart-shaped red berry (strawberry).

Another story with a similar theme is that of water lily. Water Lily was the young woman for whom Zeegwun and Bebon fought. Water Lily's parents distressed by the wrangling of their daughter's suitors removed her from land and built her a home in a bay. There the young lady lived despondent; and despondent she died. But in her state, her soul-spirit in upheaval, she was not allowed to enter the Land of Peace. The girl returned to the Land of the Living as a water lily, protected by a hair snake, as a memorial of the principle that love cannot be attained through battle.

MANDAMIN

There is another tale entitled "Corn" that is no less striking. But the story is not really about corn or its origins. It bears several themes. One of the themes is the continuation of life in a new form in the Land of the Living after death.

In a negative way the story explains the origin of corn. The term corn or maize, "Mandamin" is itself illuminating. The word Mandamin is from manda (wonder) and meen (seed or berry). Together they form a term meaning Food of Wonder.

According to the terms of the story, Mandamin was a stranger. The detail simply expresses the fact that maize is not native to the area. In the story the food is represented by an alien, a man wondrous. That the food is wondrous is expressed by the name given to it. For maize, unlike other plants, requires man's constant care in order to grow and thrive; it is capable of many food forms; and of all foods, it is the most constant for the Anishnabeg.

Zhowmin (Grape) was an orphan. His grandmother, Zhaw-b'noh-quae adopted and raised him.

When Zhowmin was about seven years old and ready to learn hunting and fishing he went to his uncles for instructions. Each day he learned from his uncles what would make him resourceful and be a good provider. He also learned to be a good warrior. From his grandmother, Zhowmin learned about the principles of life. To her the good life was not less important than the practical.

Every evening Zhaw-b'noh-quae told her grandson stories. Sometimes she told stories of acts of courage, generosity, fortitude, resourcefulness, patience, endurance, and perseverance; she sometimes related tales of the origin, purpose, and nature of things; and at other times she explained to the young boy about the laws that governed men's lives and conduct.

In the former accounts there were basic themes: "Always tell the truth;" "respect your elders;" "honour our grandfathers;" "always be thankful for food, be it scarce or abundant;" "always be thankful for life;" "always be thankful for your powers, great and small;" "seek peace;" "listen to your elders, and you will learn something;" "seek wisdom and you will do what is right;" "someday do something for your people." No matter how often Zhowmin heard these principles, he never tired of them. And because they were delivered with love, Zhowmin determined to live by these laws.

By the time Zhowmin reached manhood, his grandmother was very old and feeble. Just as she had looked after him, Zhowmin now looked after his grandmother.

Even though Zhowmin was now a man he listened to the tales recounted by his grandmother. One night after Zhaw-b'noh-quae had spoken of the "Four Hills of Life," she said, "I shall be going on a long journey, soon." Zhowmin listened, somewhat puzzled by her reference to a journey. The old lady continued, "After I leave, a stranger will come to you. Do what he says."

Zhowmin replied, "Yes, grandmother."

Before spring, Zhaw-b'noh-quae died. It was then that Zhowmin understood what his grandmother meant by a long journey. When Zhowmin and the people of the village buried Zhaw-b'noh-quae among the pines, four days after her death, her body faced the west, Man's Last Destiny.

Not long after Zhaw-b'noh-quae's death, a stranger arrived in the village and in a surly tone and petulant manner, demanded to know if there were any good men in the village.

At the demand the village elders consulted one another.

They sent for Zhowmin and presented him as a good man to the visitor.

Zhowmin took the stranger to his lodge, for they were of the same totem and Zhowmin was bound to look after him as a brother. He fed the stranger and then they smoked. Only then did Zhowmin ask the stranger the purpose of his visit.

The stranger replied, "I have been sent to find a good man. But in all my years of quest, I have not yet found one among all the peoples I have visited. I understand from your reputation that you may be such a man. I hope for your sake and for the good of your people that you are a good man."

Zhowmin rather angrily countered, "You flatter me." He asked, "Who are you? Who sent you?"

The stranger answered. "I'm Mandamin (Food of Wonder). I was sent by Kitche Manitou. My purpose is to find a good man and to test his worth. I must therefore test your strength to learn whether you or your people are worthy. And the most fitting way to test your inner strength is through battle. Zhowmin! You must fight me to prove your merit. If you win, you live; if you lose, you die."

Zhowmin scoffed, "I don't have to prove myself to you or anyone else."

Mandamin appeared disappointed. He said, "If you do not wish to fight me, I will take your refusal as cowardice. Cowardice is tantamount to defeat. In either case, there is death and it matters little whether you refuse or accept the challenge. I will still live, but I must report to Kitche Manitou that I have not found a single good man among the Anishnabeg."

That his courage and worth were doubted mattered little to Zhowmin; but that the overall merit of the Anishnabeg was questioned angered him. Then Zhowmin remembered his grandmother's words, "After I leave, a stranger will come to you. Do what he says." Partly in anger and partly out of obedience, Zhowmin glared at Mandamin, "I am not afraid. I will fight," he growled.

"Good," Mandamin said, "Tonight we'll fight." Zhowmin and Mandamin went into the forest, selected a clearing for their battle and then stripped to the waist. First they circled one another, looking for a weakness and an opening. They then grappled. Equal in determination and strength they fought on equal terms; wrestling, punching, pounding, and twisting in order to gain advantage. One moment Zhowmin would knock Mandamin to the ground; the next, Mandamin would hurl Zhowmin to the earth. So the battle went all night until both warriors fell exhausted to the soil. Zhowmin and Mandamin, bleeding and bruised returned to the lodge to rest and sleep. They slept all day.

When they awakened, it was evening. Hungry, they made a meal and ate as if there was no enmity between them. After a smoke they went back to the forest clearing to resume their struggle. Again they fought and they fought like life-long enemies. Such was the violence of their struggle that they uprooted small trees and crushed all the grasses until only the sands remained. But in spite of all their efforts neither could overcome the other. Finally, weariness forced Zhowmin and Mandamin to suspend their mighty battle. Battered, cut, and wounded, the warriors returned to their lodge to sleep.

Weak and drawn from loss of blood, they woke up late in the afternoon, ate, and then rested to regain some strength. About midnight, they slowly made their way back to the battle-ground.

Once there, they fought as hard as their remaining strength enabled them. Arms were weak; legs feeble; only the knowledge that the loser was to die kept them going. Somehow, some way, during the struggle Zhowmin knocked Mandamin to the ground; and before the unfortunate stranger could rise to his feet Zhowmin struck him with his war club. As Mandamin slumped down, Zhowmin plunged his knife into Mandamin's back. Mandamin moved no more; he was dead.

Zhowmin was remorseful. He wept beside the body of the stranger. Then he sang song for him.

"I do not fear death
My time has come
I will walk the Path of Souls
Back to whence I came."

In sorrow Zhowmin picked up the body of Mandamin and took it to the burial place where he buried the body beside that of his grandmother. Immediately afterwards he went to a medicine man to whom he related the events of the previous three days.

But the medicine man didn't say much except, "It is good that you listened to your grandmother. Look after Mandamin's grave as you would your grandmother's."

Zhowmin did as instructed. Each day he went to the grave to bring offerings and to give prayers of thanks and sorrow.

Such was the way Zhowmin honoured the dead and obeyed his grandmother and the medicine man.

One evening in late spring Zhowmin, having just brought his offerings to the graves, noticed a strange plant growing in the very centre of Mandamin's grave. Never having seen such a plant before, he examined the plant closely, but for all his knowledge of plants, he was unable to recognize it. As soon as he returned to the village, Zhowmin ran to the medicine man's lodge to report the growth of the strange plant.

As it was then too dark, the medicine man and Zhowmin decided to inspect the plant the next morning. The next morning both went. The medicine man looked at the plant, smelled it, felt its texture, but he was unable to say what the plant was. He could only advise Zhowmin to look after the plant and the graves.

June gave way to July; the strange plant grew. July yielded to August; the new plant surpassed the height of man, as slender as a pine and crowned by a tuft of hair like a tassel.

Once more the medicine man inspected the new plant. In so doing, he plucked open the leaves to determine whether the plant was good or evil.

The medicine man stripped open the wrappings until the kernels in their yellow were exposed. Deliberately, the medicine man took a kernel and placed it in his mouth.

Saying, "it is sweet, it is good," he handed a kernel to Zhowmin. Both were amazed.

The medicine man said to Zhowmin that the plant was "Mandamin, Food of Wonder. You have done a great service for your people. Be glad. You have not killed Mandamin; you have given him life in a new form. By his death, he has given life to the Anishnabeg, you and the people have been rewarded for your obedience. You have demonstrated the worth of the Anishnabeg."

LADY'S SLIPPERS

Of equal depth is the story of Lady's Slippers.

A certain village was visited by a dread disease. Even the medicine man died; and with his death all hope vanished.

Although the delivery of messages in winter was unheard of and had never before been attempted the chief asked his mizhinihway (messenger) to go to the next village for some medicines.

In those days each chief had a messenger who delivered notices and messages to distant places. Journeys even in summer were difficult; unheard of during the winter when there were no moccasins.

Nevertheless Koo-Koo-Lee prepared to go. But like the rest, he too fell ill. His wife, anxious for his life, left the lodge and slipped out into the cold. Oblivious to the cold, almost indifferent to the snow crusts, and anxious only to get medicines for her husband and the people of her village, Koo-Koo-Lee's wife ran swiftly over the drifts.

The next morning the people of the village were startled to hear her cries coming from the forest. "Koo-Koo-Lee; come and get me."

Men and women recognizing her voice ran out into the forest where they found her lying in the snow, her feet swollen and bleeding from frost bite, but the medicines in her bundle for her husband and the rest of the sick people in the village. The men carried her back to her lodge and wrapped her feet in thick warm deer skins.

For her sacrifice to her husband and devotion to her people, she was named thereafter Wah-on-nay. On her death her foot wrappings became little flowers of yellow, called by some Wah-on-nay moccasinun; by others Koo-Koo-Lee moccasinun. They are also known as Lady's Slippers.

THE GOOD OF PLANTS

Plants have many purposes, all of them good. Some sustain men in their growth and existence; some heal; others give beauty and inner strength.

As Food

Foods were discovered by observation and deduction, some quite by accident.

For example. That the fluids of trees were nutritious was discovered, according to tradition, in the following manner.

The birch tree suffered enormously from the itch, he squirmed; he writhed in discomfort. Though he had numerous limbs, arms, and fingers, he could not scratch. There was nothing the birch tree could do to relieve his sufferings.

In his agony the poor birch called out to the squirrels and porcupines and beavers to pick out the ticks, grubs, and beetles that were tormenting him. But the squirrels and porcupines and beavers were too busy to offer any help. The best they could do was to give their sympathy without limit.

Next the birch called out to the birds. They too felt sorry for the birch, but they could do nothing. Only the woodpeckers came to help. Coming to the aid of the poor tree the downy woodpecker, his cousin, the red-headed woodpecker, the flicker, and the chickadee all picked every pest from beneath the bark of the birch. The birch tree ceased itching.

Many years later the woodpeckers were in distress. Not

knowing what to do or from whom they could find help, they, at last came to the birch and related a sad story. In the long rainless spell, the woodpeckers were dying from thirst. The woodpeckers were unable to drink from pools and lakes and streams, like other birds could.

"Could," they asked, "you do something?"

The birch remembering the help that he had received from the woodpeckers said to them, "Go to my trunk and drill two holes near each other and they will presently fill up with my sap."

The desperate woodpeckers flew down and drummed away at the trunk of the tree, until they had drilled two tiny holes. Almost immediately the holes began to fill up and yield a rich flow of sap. Thirstily, the woodpeckers drank and they have been drinking from trees since that time.

From the woodpeckers the Anishnabeg learned that trees yield sap and that trees could be tapped. Like the woodpecker, the Anishnabeg tapped the birch for a vinegar tasting drink and later tapped the maple for a sweet drink.

The story of the discovery of maple sugar depicts accidental learning.

It seems that a young bride, somewhat lazy and absent-minded was fond of visiting her neighbours to gossip. Instead of fetching good water for use in her cooking she often poured maple sap into her pot of stew. Then, while her stew simmered she would leave to chatter with her friends. Most often she came home on time to remove the food from the fireplace. As a result of her daily excursions away from her lodge she gained a reputation for laziness.

"Someday, something is going to happen," the elders said sadly. They watched and waited.

They waited quite awhile, but the day of reckoning eventually came. As was her habit the young bride began her meal preparation early in the afternoon while her husband was away hunting. As soon as she had made venison stew in maple sap she went to her neighbours to talk. In the gossip exchange she forgot her stew.

As the sun sank beyond the hills, the husband came home bearing a deer. Depositing the game at the doorway, he called out to his wife, "I'm hungry. I've brought home another deer."

But he received no answer. He called again and looked into the lodge. She was gone. Angrily he called out once more thinking that perhaps his wife was nearby gathering firewood. He looked over to the fireplace. Only the pot hung over a heap of grey ashes; the fire had long since expired.

The hungry and weary husband grew angrier. No wife; no meal. He walked over to the pot, looked inside; there was only burnt venison. He was furious; he would, he resolved, punish his wife. However, because he was ferociously hungry, he dipped his hand into the pot and extracted a black, sticky mass of meat which he placed in his mouth. How good and firm; moreover it was sweet. His mood changed, as he reached for more. Anger was replaced by joy. In a short while, he had nearly demolished the venison stew.

He was not only glad he was also proud of the cleverness of his wife who had created such a delicious and marvellous dish. She may, he thought, be somewhat lazy and forgetful, but she was not without resourcefulness.

The hunter went in search of his wife. He went from lodge to lodge asking for her, but no one would volunteer to say where she might be. Usually, they would tell him without much prompting. But this time no one wanted to be the one who would tell of her whereabouts and be the instrument of his rage. Eventually, without anyone's help he found his wife hiding and trembling in her mother's lodge. The girl's mother too was quaking.

As the hunter poked his head into the lodge he smiled saying, "I've never eaten such a wonderful meal as I've had tonight. How did you cook it?" The bride was puzzled and her fear diminished. The hunter said, "Come." The bride followed.

When they got home she tasted the remains of the stew. Then she understood.

In story form, the Anishnabeg explained how they discovered maple syrup and maple sugar quite by accident.

As Medicine
Some plants heal.

That plants possess curative properties was deduced from the relationship between animals and birds and plants. The healing powers of plants were found in a manner similar to the following account.

A little girl and her grandmother were out picking blueberries. As they made their way along the lush patches of berries, the grandmother abruptly halted, pointed to the ground, and whispered to her granddaughter, "Watch, you will never see this again."

The little girl looked to the ground where her grandmother pointed. There in the grasses was a snake pursuing a small green frog. Little girl and aged woman watched the drama on the ground. The snake was gaining but before he could seize the frog in his jaws, the frightened quarry leaped into a grove of poison ivy.

In the growth of poison ivy, the little frog waited, his sides heaving with exertion. He appeared unconcerned, not seeking more cover or further refuge. The snake did not enter the poison ivy but coiled himself as if he were going to strike out at the little frog in his sanctuary. But the snake, tongue darting in and out of his jaws, remained poised, not daring to go closer. He simply waited for the frog to come out. But the little frog did not move. At length, certain but disappoined that his victim would not leave his haven, the snake crawled slowly away. Even with the departure of the snake, the frog did not immediately vacate his shelter. Only after he was sure that the snake had abandoned his enterprise did the frog leave his place of security.

Once out of the poison ivy the little frog fairly flew over the ground bounding without pause until he came to another grove of plants. Within that grove of jewel weed, the little frog twisted and turned and writhed washing every part of himself.

From the conduct of the little frog the Anishnabeg learned the cure for poison ivy.

Similarly were the properties of other plants discovered. The Anishnabeg found that the root of a certain plant ingested, will terminate a haemorrhage; that the soft waxen substance between bark and wood of cedar will stop external bleeding; that the leaf of cedar or balsam will form a brew when boiled that will relieve throat congestion; that the swamp root called jeebkae will relieve throat pains; and that large flat grass leaves will alleviate abrasions.

The healing power of plants could relieve physical pain and confer well being. But many medicine men and women knew that many forms of ill health were but outward manifestations and forms of the poor state of inner being. There was a recognition that there was a relationship between the physical well being of a person and his inner well being; illness and inner turmoil.

Consequently, in addition to the application of medicines to hurts, a state of peace had to be instilled in the inner being of a patient.

As Ceremonial Substance

Nourishing as are the fruits of trees and plants; soothing to injuries as are roots and saps; yet beautiful are plants to man's spirit and his senses.

There was in the Anishnabeg, an inclination toward peace; there was a need to touch Kitche Manitou. Of all plants none was more suitable than was tobacco for inducing peace or transporting man's thoughts and prayers to Kitche Manitou.

In the first place tobacco was a gift of the spirit. It was the father of Nanabush who gave the tobacco and shared the custom of smoking with his son after their epic battle as a symbol of peace. Nanabush in turn passed on the custom to the Anishnabeg as a ceremony. Thereafter, the Anishnabeg smoked the Pipe of Peace before great councils, after war, and before other ceremonies. The Anishnabeg adopted the custom and made it part of their daily lives to compose their minds and spirits. What had been given had to be perpetuated.

In the second place tobacco was in the nature of an incense sweet to the taste and fragrant to smell. No other plant is endowed with such qualities.

In the third place, tobacco is a natural child of Mother Earth and Father Sun, the natural victim to be offered in sacrifice in the smoking of the Pipe of Peace. It was central to the ceremony. The leaf comes to an end; and commingled with the breath of life is borne skyward to Kitche Manitou. What is given by the giver is returned in symbol of gratitude by the recipient. Through immolation, tobacco a tangible, sensible, substance represented the union between man and his God; and prefigured man's own final destiny.

There were few ceremonies in winter. When spring came so were the ceremonies revived. For in spring, occurred life's greatest drama; birth, re-birth, and renewal. It was the time during which man himself emerged from the ordeal of winter. Becoming and youth were imaged in everything. And the predominant colour of birth and becoming and renewal was green; it became the colour of life itself.

Though green ultimately becomes yellow and then brown, green remains the colour of life. As it images youth, a transitory stage in life, so the shade of the evergreen means continuity. While other shades of green come to an end; the green of cedar and spruce and pine abide through the winters. For the Anishnabeg, green meant life, life giving, and life sustenance.

THE PRIMACY OF PLANTS

Plants can exist alone; but neither animals nor men can exist without plants. Without plants, or when their balance is disturbed, the quality of life and existence declines.

To illustrate man's dependence upon the plant world and to show how delicate is the fabric of dependence and interdependence and how fragile the balance, the Anishnabeg told the following story.

Roses were once the most numerous and brilliantly coloured of all the flowers. Such were their numbers and such were the variety and richness of their shades that they were common. No one paid much attention to them; their beauty went unnoticed, their glory unsung.

Even when their numbers declined and their colours faded, no one appeared to care. Cycles of scarcity and plenty had occurred. There was no cause for alarm. There is degeneration and regeneration. Plenty always follows scarcity.

But year after year roses became fewer in number. As the numbers and richness of the flowers diminished, the fatness of the rabbits increased. Only the bear, and the bee, and the humming-bird were aware that something was wrong.

The Anishnabeg felt that something was not quite right but they couldn't explain it. They only knew that the bear was thinner and that the bear's flesh was less sweet than formerly. The bears found smaller quantities of honey and what they found was less delectable. The bees and humming-birds found fewer roses. The Anishnabeg were bewildered; the bears blamed the bees; the bees were alarmed. But no one could do anything.

Eventually, one summer there were no roses. Bees hungered; humming-birds grew thin; the bears raged. In later years, that summer was known as the Summer of the Disappearance of the Rose. At last, everyone was alarmed. In desperation, a great meeting was called. Everyone was invited.

There were many days of discussion before the meeting decided to dispatch all the swift to search the world for a single rose; and, if they found one, to bring it back. Months went by before a humming-bird chanced to discover a solitary rose growing and clinging to a mountainside in a far off land.

The humming-bird lifted the faint and pallid rose from its bed and brought it back. On arrival, medicine men and women immediately tended the rose and in a few days restored the rose to life. When he was well enough the rose was able to give an account of the destruction of the roses.

In a voice quivering with weakness, the rose said, "The rabbits ate all the roses."

The assembly raised an angry uproar. At the word, the bears and wolves and lynxes seized the rabbits by the ears and cuffed them around. During the assault the rabbits' ears were stretched and their mouths were split open. The outraged animals might have killed all the rabbits that day had not the rose interceded on their behalf saying, "Had you cared and

44

watched us, we might have survived. But you were unconcerned. Our destruction was partly your fault. Leave the rabbits be."

Reluctantly the angry animals released the rabbits. While the rabbits wounds eventually healed, they did not lose their scars which remained as marks of their intemperance. Nor did the roses ever attain their former brilliance or abundance. Instead the roses received from Nanabush thorns to protect them from the avarice of the hungry and the intemperate.

Nanabush, in endowing the roses with thorns, warned the assembly, "You can take the life of plants; but you cannot give them life."

The Nature of Animals

OUR ELDER BROTHERS

Third in the order of creation were the animal beings. There
were those who flew, those who swam, those who crawled, and
those who walked.

From the very first, all animals possessed a special affinity
with Mother Earth and with plants. They lived by the Great
Laws and they somehow had a precognition or pre-knowledge
of events.

Besides this great gift, which all possessed, each species
and each individual creature was endowed with unique and
singular powers proper to himself and his kind. Each had his
sphere on earth, each his own time for the performance and
fulfilment of his purpose and powers. Such was the general
nature of animal beings.

In the beginning, animals were created without powers.
They were required to approach Kitche Manitou on a high
mountain to receive his gifts.

The eagle received strong wings, keen sight, and aloofness.
His sphere was the mountain and the heights. He was content.

To the humming-bird was given the power of hovering.
He was entrusted with tending the flowers and blossoms. As
his nourishment the humming-bird was to feed upon the sweet
nectars and to share them with the bees. He was content.

Kitche Manitou gave to the vulture flight, and patience,
and watchfulness. His task was to keep the meadows clean and
the wind pure. He, too, was content.

The bear received strength; the otter, playfulness; the
butterfly, beauty; the tadpole, transformation; the dog, a loving

nature; the beaver, peace; the wolf, fidelity; the fox, resourcefulness; the owl, care; the deer, grace; the trout, fertility. All animal beings received a portion of the power of Kitche Manitou; and most were content.

Only the wolverine was discontented. When he saw the extent of the gifts of the other animals, he grew envious. Soon he wanted the strength and the size of a bear, the elegance of deer, and the swiftness of the fox. In his increasing disappointment, the wolverine began to despise himself and his gifts and feel bitter at Kitche Manitou. At length, he resolved to return to the mountain top and ask the Master of Life for greater and better gifts.

When the wolverine attained the crest, he boldly called out, "Kitche Manitou! Hear me! You have not been just to me. You have not been just to all the animals. To some you have given greater scope and a greater measure of gifts. By this uneven distribution you have made some great and some less."

More audacious, the wolverine continued, "I demand that you redress this great wrong. For myself, I wish more strength, more comeliness, more speed."

But Kitche Manitou's thunderous voice broke through the selfish list of wolverine. "To each animal being I have given sufficient power for the fulfilment of his being and form. The power I have conferred on each is a form of my power, and is a reflection of my gifts.

"No injustice has been done. If you have not developed and fostered the gifts I have presented to you, it is you who have perpetrated an injustice upon yourself. You have betrayed yourself.

"For your presumption, you shall wander alone and despised. And for your refusal to develop your attributes you will, henceforth, feed upon what has been left over by your fellow creatures who have nurtured their talents. Go!"

Wolverine left the mountain top more bitter and envious than before. He had not been daunted by Kitche Manitou himself!

As Kitche Manitou ordained, so the wolverine became solitary, vicious, and avoided. Hungry ever, he must feed upon the portions left by other animals.

Very different was the manner of the snake upon receiving his form and powers. Legless, armless, and wingless, he nevertheless kept the little plants in the fields and meadows safe. Not once did he complain of his condition or covet the better fortune of others. Cheerful and satisfied he made the most of his least of powers.

Unfortunately for the poor snake and his brothers, there were rabbits, the most mischievous of creatures. While the snakes could repel the smaller rodents from the gardens, they were unable to discourage the fleet and numerous rabbits. The ordeal for the snakes began not out of evil or malice on the part of the rabbits, but arose out of the playful dispositions of the long-eareds, and their voracious appetites.

The rabbits ate and ate. Try as they might the snakes were unable to prevent the rabbits from destroying plants and gardens. Instead of selecting a few succulent leaves from each plant, so that more leaves could grow and the plants benefit, the greedy rabbits ate all the leaves, the stalks, the flowers, and often, the roots as well. They stripped the bark from seedling trees. No plant was safe from them. The snakes warned and fought as best they could; the rabbits merely snickered, and ate some more.

Discovering that snakes were feeble, the rabbits made sport of them. In play the rabbits pulled their tails, sat on them, dragged them around, and even tossed them in the air. The snakes were helpless; they suffered injuries and indignities. In their grief and to bring their torments to an end, the snakes pleaded with the rabbits to stop. It was useless.

At last, wearying of the abuse heaped upon them, the snakes called upon Kitche Manitou for help.

They went to the Mountain of Gifts where they called out to Kitche Manitou, "Hear us, Kitche Manitou! We are oppressed. The rabbits have inflicted harms and insults upon us. We are defenceless against them; we cannot fulfil our duties to the plant beings. Kitche Manitou, help us!"

Kitche Manitou took pity on the poor snakes. He gave some of them venom, and to others the ability to wrap themselves tightly around creatures and crush them. He warned them: "Do not abuse the power I have given to you. Use it as a last resort; use it properly. Before resorting to poison warn your enemies, and perhaps, by a threat, you can avoid destroying other creatures."

The snakes thanked Kitche Manitou for the additional gifts and then returned to their homes.

Before long the other animal beings learned of the potency of the snake.

A rabbit was in a merry mood. Watched by his brothers, he began to tease the snake who was busy guarding a corn field.

It began harmlessly enough. Rabbit blocked the snake's way, pulled at his tail, and nipped him behind the head. Such treatment did not hurt the snake but prevented him from carrying out his duties, and gave insult to his dignity as a guardian. Still, he said nothing. Soon the merriment grew abusive. Rabbit cuffed, then picked up the snake and tossed him into the air. The snake fell to the ground dazed and bleeding.

"That's enough. No more," the snake hissed, rattling his tail in anger.

Rabbit laughed; the other rabbits chortled. "An empty threat. Threats ought not to be made by one incapable of carrying them out," smirked the rabbit as he darted toward the coiled snake.

The snake lashed out and sank his fangs deep into the rabbit's nose. Rabbit jumped back, reeled, and fell to the ground. He moved no more. The other watching rabbits fled in terror.

Such stories reflect the composite nature of all animal beings. Each member is made up of two substances; one corporeal; the other, incorporeal. The scope and nature of the soul-spirit of an animal is expressed in his mood and temperament. Perhaps deeper than this is the certain belief that the power of a creature was an extension of Kitche Manitou's powers conferred in an animal creature. Implicit too, is the suggestion that physical forms limit and constrain the incorporeal.

The animal beings lived in concord with the laws of the world. Initially, they lived in harmony with one another and with all beings, subject to the same laws of nature. It is said they understood one another.

MAN'S DEPENDENCE ON ANIMALS

When the world was flooded, all the land animals perished; only the fishes and birds and animals who lived in the water survived.

With their prescience and preknowledge, the animals sensed the supernatural conception of man in the spirit-woman. It was their feeling of compassion for the spirit woman that prompted the animals to invite her down to rest upon the turtle's back. Even the smallest and the least of the animals, the muskrat, served. When all the others failed, the muskrat brought back from the bottom of the sea the small portion of soil requested by the spirit woman. Without the animals the world would not have been; without the animals the world would not be intelligible.

At birth man was helpless. Again it was the animals who assisted the spirit woman in nourishing the newborn infants by bringing fruits, vegetables, berries, and drink, while the birds and butterflies brought joy.

That winter, when food was scarce and the winds cold, the

animals sheltered man. The bear, who loved the newborn beings, offered his flesh so that the Anishnabeg would survive. Following the example of the bear, the deer, moose, porcupine, beaver, ground hog, grouse, and goose, and almost every animal being offered himself in sacrifice.

Even when the first man and woman were fully grown and had many descendants, the animals continued to serve. Man relied on the creatures for all his needs. He did not work because there was no need for labour. Life was easy. More and more the Anishnabeg relied upon the animals. And as life was easy for mankind, it was difficult for the animal beings. The animals' burdens became more onerous.

Men and women understood the utterances of the animals; the animals understood man. It was this mutual understanding that enabled man to impose greater burdens upon his brothers. What was worse, man set animal against animal.

Instead of doing his own fishing, man dispatched a loon or a kingfisher to catch fish for him. If he wanted a rabbit, man would send an eagle or a hawk; if he wanted a partridge, he would send a fox; if he wanted the sap of trees, he ordered the woodpecker to drill holes in the trees for him; if he wanted a new lodge, he commanded the beaver and the porcupine to fell the trees. The animals did all the work; man did none.

For a long time the animals served without complaint. But what was worse than burdens was the apparent indifference of the Anishnabeg to the needs of the animals themselves. Little could be collected and stored to keep them during the long winter, and what was set aside, was often taken by man. Service brought poverty.

At last, weary of service, the animals convened a great meeting to gain their freedom. All came at the invitation of the courier.

The bear was chosen to be the first speaker and to act as chairman of the session. He explained the purpose of the meeting. "We are met to decide our destiny. We have been oppressed far too long by man. He has taken our generosity and repaid us with ingratitude; he has taken our labours and repaid us with servitude; he has taken our friendship and fostered enmity among us.

"Either we continue to serve him or we withhold our labours. Are we to continue to serve? We shall come to an end. If we deny our labours we shall live. Should you choose the former, you must resign yourselves to your fate. Should you prefer the latter, then you must consider the manner by which it is to be accomplished. Consider carefully."

The bear had scarcely finished when the groundhog shouted out, "I am for man's death. We have suffered enough. The Anishnabeg have killed us; they have been unkind; and they have subjected us. Only with the death of man will these injustices cease. Man must die."

"Hey! Hey! Let him die," concurred the animals.

"I am for life. I am for mercy," said the dog on rising. "While, it is true, that man has been unkind, he has not been unkind to all. There are many in this company who have not suffered. The cat, the vulture, the whippoorwill, the frog, the butterfly, the mouse, the humming-bird have, all of them, lived and worked, and rested without harm. To them man has been kind. Perhaps he has been somewhat thoughtless. Is this a good reason to wish him dead? Man does not deserve death; he deserves to live, even as we live."

"Hey! Hey! Let him live," chorused the dog's supporters.

The wolverine rose to his feet, visage dark and threatening. "Let the Anishnabeg neither live or die, but let him suffer. If you have suffered at man's hand you are partly to blame; for he who allows himself to be servile deserves servitude. He bears as much guilt as he who subjects. Man is not entirely to blame, and ought not pay the entire penalty for your folly."

As he sat down, the wolverine taunted, "And if man is to die, who will kill him?"

The meeting buzzed with the consternation of the animals. Questions were asked, "If man is to die, who will kill him?"

All the animals looked at one another, but not one spoke to answer this final question.

"Bear, will you kill him?" asked the wolverine sardonically.

"Yes! The bear! He is strong and brave," shouted the animals.

The bear cringed, turning somewhat grey. "I am too slow. I am unwilling. There are too few of us," he replied to excuse himself.

"Then the wolves must do it. They are fast and strong," offered the wolverine.

Not expecting to be named, the startled wolves managed to sputter, "We cannot, and we dare not. Man is too clever."

"Cowards!" jeered the wolverine. "The rattlesnake shall do it."

But the rattlesnakes refused saying, "We are too slow. Man is too swift. We are not big enough."

While the debate raged, a dog stole away from the meeting. A vigilant wolf spied him and trailed him.

The debate continued and became a clamour. The bear, realizing that nothing could be resolved with opinion divided and feelings heated, called the meeting to order. "We cannot kill man. He is too strong, too many, and too cunning. Nor should we want to kill him or injure him. He, too, is entitled to life and well being. We can resolve our state without man's death."

It was at this time that the wolf dragged the errant dog into the meeting and near the central fire.

Without waiting to be asked to speak, the wolf angrily shouted above the din. The whimpering of the dog and the ululating snarl of the wolf instilled silence.

"This dog has betrayed us. He must be punished. A little while ago he made off almost unnoticed. But I saw him and followed. He went directly to the village of the Anishnabeg and divulged what we were discussing. This one and all the dogs must be punished."

The assembled animals were outraged. They seized the dogs and began to pummel them. But though the bear was as outraged as his brothers, he maintained his composure. He thundered out, "Brothers, it is too late. To kill the dogs would be without purpose and substance. Rather let him endure his servitude. Let him serve man. Let him hunger. Let him hunt for man. Let him guard man. Let him know man's fickleness."

Turning to the dog, the bear speaking on behalf of his brothers said, "For your betrayal, you shall no longer be regarded as a brother among us. Instead of man, we shall attack you. Worse than this, from now on you shall eat only what man has left, sleep in the cold and rain, and receive kicks as a reward for your fidelity."

The bear turned again to the crowd. "To make it difficult for man to enslave us again, no longer will we speak the same language. Instead we shall speak in different languages. From now on we shall live to ourselves, for ourselves. Let men learn to fend for themselves without our help."

With that the meeting broke up, and the animals went their separate ways.

Man was dependent upon the animals for his food, clothing, and tools; man was also dependent upon animals for knowledge of the world, life, and himself.

There is in animals a unique capacity to sense the changes of the world, the alteration of seasons, and the coming state of things. Man does not have the preknowledge possessed by bluebird, or trout, or squirrel. For man to prepare, he looked to his elder brothers.

Eagles, geese, and robins knew of the advent of autumn and would leave for the south. The squirrels sensed the quality of the coming winter and in preparation played less, stored large quantities of provisions, and made deep dens. What bees sensed, dictated how high or how low they built their nests, and how much honey they would produce. Bluebirds and robins knew when to return to their summering grounds. Men did not possess this faculty. Not having it, they had to find preknowledge through the animal beings.

There was another aspect to animal beings. They possessed and reflected character, the external manifestation of the elemental nature and quality of the inner being.

Animals became the totemic symbols of the Anishnabeg.

CRANE	— eloquence for leadership
HAWK	— deliberation, foresight
EAGLE	— courage, preknowledge
SEAGULL	— grace, peace
LOON	— fidelity
EAGLE (White headed)	— foresight
BLACK DUCK	— depth
GOOSE	— prudence
SPARROW HAWK	— perseverance
BEAR	— strength and courage
MARTEN	— single mindedness; judgement
MOOSE	— endurance, strength
CARIBOU	— grace and watchfulness
WOLF	— perseverance, guardianship
LYNX	— resolution, fortitude
BEAVER	— resourcefulness, mind own business
MUSKRAT	— endurance
PIKE	— swiftness, elegance
SUCKER	— calmness, grace
STURGEON	— depth, strength
WHITE FISH	— abundance, fertility, beauty
MERMAID (MERMAN)	— temptation
FROG	— transformation
WATER SNAKE	— willingness
TURTLE	— communication, emissary
RATTLESNAKE	— patience, slow to anger
CATFISH	— breadth, scope

As these animals were endowed with certain traits of character, so did the Anishnabeg endeavour to emulate that character, and make it part of themselves. Each animal symbolized an ideal to be sought, attained, and perpetuated.

THE LOONS

What force
Brought you together
Your destinies to unite?
Chance?
Nature?

What element
Cleaves one your souls
In their separate beings?
Will?
Nature?

What purpose
Impels your spirits one
Alone to range the realms?
Freedom?
Nature?

What depths
Move your hearts
To trumpet summons "return?"
Feeling
Nature only?

What powers
Draws you in fidelity
To endure in harmony one?
Love?
Nature?

THE SNAKE

A chilling chafing rattle
Somewhere on the forest floor
Bestirs terrors new and old
In my hollow, craven chest.

O, hidden, fatal serpent
Are you poised and coiled for sting?
Or are you like me, afraid
And quiver out of mere dread?

But fears real and fancied
Still remain and will not go
And at each new crisis come
Will well and my heart constrict.

In you hurtful and deadly
Shall I seek what I have not
And like the Hopi through you
Compose and dispel all dreads.

When foolish, mawkish fears
Unchain themselves and leave me free
My heart not warring with my mind
Then peace will my being have.

THE EAGLE

Mighty Eagle
I fain would see my destiny
And know my impending fates
To live my life in harmony
With fortune, chances, and states.
But I scarce know the days event.
I cannot see o'er the rim,
I cannot see o'er the present,
Into the ages far and dim.

Mighty Eagle
In vain I scan the past
For signs and marks sharp and clear
To guide my way into the last.
But memory faded by the year,
Confounds what was with what was not;
Blends fact and fancy into one
Fickle and beclouded lot,
Fouling steps that must be done.

Mighty Eagle
I deign would have your powers
Of vision, strength and courage
To wield against the unborn hours
Of troubles upon my pilgrimage.
My spirit seeking fulness,
And heart tending toward peace,
My deeds done in goodness;
Then, would my worth find increase.

Animals were more than flesh for food, more than the re-
flections of coming changes, and more than images of character.
They were living beings entitled to life and existence. But for
men to live, the animal beings had to die.

To acknowledge their dependence upon the animal beings

for almost all aspects of life, the Anishnabeg included them in almost all their stories.

Such was the totality of that dependence that the Anishnabeg related stories of the disappearance of animals and tried to conceive the consequences that would follow. Perhaps the annual departure of animals prompted such stories. Even if this were the case, the fact remains that with the departure of the animal beings, the quality and the tone of life changed.

For some inexplicable reason the deer, the moose, and the caribou once vanished from the land of the Anishnabeg. With their going, the life of the Anishnabeg was not what it had been. To restore the quality of life the Anishnabeg went in search of them.

Assisted by the other animal beings whose state of being, too, had been altered, the Anishnabeg roamed the world in quest of the vanished animals. An owl, who had gone north more in search of rest than labour, came upon the herd confined in an immense enclosure as if imprisoned. Yet they seemed quite content, grazing upon the spruces, pines, cedars, and balsams.

Curious, the owl flew down to a low hanging branch to question the deer. But as he alighted upon the branch, a flock of crows attacked him and drove him from the country. The owl barely got away. That it was night, no doubt, enabled the owl to escape. The owl left the land as fast as he could.

Back in the land of the Anishnabeg, the owl reported his discovery immediately. The Anishnabeg speedily organized a large war party to rescue the imprisoned deer. Owl guided the expedition.

When the war party arrived at the very gates of the enclosure, it was attacked by a vast flock of fierce crows. Days of battle followed with neither side victorious. The Anishnabeg fought ferociously; the crows stormed relentlessly. But at no time during the conflict did the deer attempt to escape; they simply looked on in curiosity. Their seeming indifference dismayed the invaders.

Discouraged, the Anishnabeg asked for a truce. The crows granted the request, and looked on smugly as the chief of the Anishnabeg addressed the deer. "Why are you unconcerned with our efforts to rescue you from your enforced confinement? We have endured hardship, and risked death on your behalf. Still you appear indifferent."

The chief of the deer replied, "You have assumed wrongly that we are here against our wishes. On the contrary, we choose to remain here and are quite content. The crows have treated us better than you have ever treated us when we shared the same country with you."

"How did we offend you?" asked the chief, astonished.

The deer chief spoke quickly and sadly. "You have wasted our flesh; you have despoiled our haunts; you have desecrated our bones; you have dishonoured us and yourselves. Without you we can live. But without us, you cannot live."

"How shall we make amends? Know that our seeming indifference was not ill will. How shall we atone for your grief? Tell us," said the Anishnabe chief.

Again the deer chief spoke. "Honour and respect our lives, our beings, in life and in death. Do what you have not done before. Cease doing what offends our spirits."

The chief promised and the crows released the deer, the moose, and the caribou from their bondage. The animals who had been in captivity willingly followed the Anishnabeg back to their homeland.

This and similar stories reflect a recurring theme in the life of the Anishnabeg and their outlook.

> All life must be honoured.
> The quality of life for one order depends upon another.
> Take life but not in anger.
> Life for one means death for another.
> By honouring death, life itself is honoured.
> Animal beings deserve life. They deserve honour.

Many animal beings quit the land for the winter; life changed for the Anishnabeg. From this annual circumstance and from the periodic disappearance of animals began many customs and practices connected with the taking of game.

There were prayers said or thought at the death of an animal being, prayers that expressed sorrow and heed and apology.

PRAYER TO A DEER SLAIN BY A HUNTER

> I had need,
> I have dispossessed you of beauty, grace, and life.
> I have sundered your spirit from its wordly frame.
> No more will you run in freedom
> Because of my need.

> I had need.
> You have in life served your kind in goodness.
> By your life, I will serve my brothers.
> Without you I hunger and grow weak.
> Without you I am helpless, nothing.

> I had need.
> Give me your flesh for strength.

Give me your casement for protection.
Give me your bones for my labours,
And I shall not want.

Not only was the primacy of animal beings acknowledged in prayer, it was memorialized in the instruments of ceremony. Attached to the sacred Pipe of Peace were the plumes of the eagle and the tegument of animal. Each of the four orders of life and being were represented in ritual. Only when the four orders were present was the instrument complete and the ceremony fulfilled. Without the four dimensions there was no unity.

In the Midewewin, animal beings, and the world of animal beings were represented. Often animal beings were represented as contraries, or contradictions. One time the bear represented good; another, he imaged evil. This portrayed a fact of being and life, that there are two aspects to everything, appearing as opposites. Birth and death, youth and old age, day and night, man and woman, water and fire, wind and rock, sadness and joy, triumph and defeat, body and soul-spirit, good and evil. That life and being are paradoxical is stated in prayer and tangibly represented in the Midewewin.

The tegument of ermine constitutes an essential portion of the medicine bag. By it the medicine man or woman is reminded that the knowledge of the curative properties of plants comes through animals.

For the third order members of the Midewewin who practised the Jeesekeewin (communion with the incorporeal world), the turtle symbolized the celerity of thought and the means by which the different dimensions and orders of beings communicated.

Other animal beings were similarly honoured in prayer and ritual.

At the practical level, animals were respected in the following ways:

Female animals with young were spared. Only males were to be taken.
Young were to be allowed to grow.
A pair of animal beings were to be allowed to live to insure continuation of life.
The bones of game were to be used, not wasted. The bones of fish were not to be cast into the water.

Such was the way the Anishnabeg endeavoured to honour the life death, and knowledge of the animal beings. Men and women called them "Our Elder Brothers."

Man's World

From man's five basic individual and social needs and endeavours, leadership, protection, sustenance, learning, and physical well being, emerged the framework and fabric of Ojibway society. It was the fulfilment of these needs for individual and social growth that formed the *raison d'être* for society. Each function in the Ojibway schemata of society, government, defense, provision of necessities, education, and medical practice, was discharged by a social unit whose members were born into the unit and especially trained. Each social unit represented one form or aspect of public duty which was symbolized by an emblem, known as a totem. The totem was probably the most important social unit taking precedence over the tribe, community, and the immediate family.

The Ojibway speaking people which included the Ottawa, Pottawatomi, Ojibway proper, and the Mississauga, and if the Sauk, Menominee, and Algonquin are to be further added make up a large tribe. Although these peoples spoke a similar language, and shared a common cultural heritage, there was no marked sense of tribal unity or identity; there was no need. Men and women preferred to regard themselves as members of a totem and then a community. Strangers, when they met, always asked one another, "Waenaesh k'dodaem?" (What is your totem?); only afterwards did they ask, "Waenaesh keen?" (Who are you?) The question and answer reflected the nature and importance of the individual and corporate sense of identity. By implication the question and manner of inquiry was intended to elicit an answer not so much as to place of birth and habitual residence, but as to band membership. The nature of the response was similar in context. When asked of their identity men and women might answer "Zaugee," or "Zaugeewinini," meaning "I am of the People of the River Mouth," or "Potta-wotomi," which means "I am of the People of the Keepers of the Fire," or "Menominee — I am of the People of the Wild Rice," or "Mitche Kuneewinini — I am of the People of the Water Fence (Rama)". In all cases the emphasis was not on the place or origin of birth, but on an affiliation, "I am of the People of . . ." Custom and practice seemed to indicate that totemic and band or community affiliation took precedence over tribe or other consideration.

The Ojibway speaking peoples constituted one of the largest tribes north of the Mexican border. Numerous bands were remote and distant from one another. Some were small comprising but a few families, while others were large consisting of many families and containing many hundreds of people.

Ideally each band would embody or incorporate the five basic social units to fulfil its functions as a community. But this was not always the case.

A band or community in which all totemic groups were represented might appear graphically in this way:

LEADERSHIP DEFENSE SUSTENANCE LEARNING MEDICINE
Chief(s)   Warriors Hunters   Teachers   Healers

Originally there were five totems representing the five needs of the people and the five elementary functions of society. Later others were added.

LEADERSHIP
Chejauk (Crane)
Wawa (Goose)
Mong (Loon)
Kaikaik (Hawk)
Peepeegizaence —
(Sparrow Hawk)
Migizi (White headed eagle)
Kineu (Black headed eagle)
Makataezheeb (Brant)
Kayaushk (Seagull)

DEFENSE
Noka (Bear)
Myeengun (Wolf)
Pizheu (Lynx)

SUSTENANCE
Waubizhaezh (Marten)
Amik (Beaver)

Moozo (Moose)
Addik (Caribou)
Wawashkaesh (Deer)
Wuzhushk (Muskrat)

LEARNING
Mizi (Catfish)
Kinozhae (Pike)
Numaebin (Sucker)
Numae (Sturgeon)
Addikmeg (Whitefish)

MEDICINE
Makinauk (Turtle)
Negik (Otter)
Medawaewae (Rattle snake)
Muzundumo (Black snake)
Mukukee (Frog)
Nebaunaube (quae) (Merman
   or mermaid)

The evidence is strong that the term "dodaem" comes from the same root as do "dodum" and "dodosh." "Dodum" means to do or fulfil, while "Dodosh," literally means breast, that from which milk, or food, or sustenance is drawn. Dodaem may mean "that from which I draw my purpose, meaning, and being."'

A legend relates the origin of the totems, six great creatures emerged from the sea. One exposed to the light and heat of the sun expired sinking back into the sea. The survivors came to shores of the Land of the Anishnabeg by whom they were welcome. In appreciation, the five incorporeal beings offered to guide the Anishnabeg in the conduct of their affairs.

DIVISIONS OF SOCIETY

Leadership

Of all echo-makers the crane was most eminent and for this reason was selected to symbolize leadership and direction. The call that he uttered was as infrequent as it was unique. So unusual was the tone and pitch of the voice that all other creatures suspended their own utterances to harken to the crane. When the crane calls, all listen.

As the crane calls infrequently and commands attention, so ought a leader exercise his prerogative rarely and bear the same attention in the discharge of his duties. He speaks infrequently lest he be considered shallow. A leader having no other source of authority except for his force of character and persuasion did not jeopardize his tenuous ability. Moreover a leader was first in action, not merely commander; as a speaker he did not utter his own sentiments, but those of his people. As such, the leader was obliged to shield the feelings of his people and not to depreciate them by too frequent speech. He was as leader an example and the first of speakers only.

Leadership was predicated upon persuasion; its exercise upon circumstances and need. It was neither permanent nor constant for a chief. Rather, it was temporary and intermittent as it was obtained in the physical world. Twice annually, once in late summer and again in early spring does the occasion arise for the exercise of leadership among the birds. Late in summer, the birds assemble in flocks under one leader to proceed to the south; in early spring, they return under the guidance of a leader. When the need is ended, so is leadership.

Even when circumstance demands leadership, the act of leading is without compulsion. The followers follow freely and are at liberty to withdraw. When the flock arrives at its destination, the members disband and terminate the conduct of leadership.

Nor do all members of the same species commit themselves to the same leader. There are many flocks formed to attain the same destination; different trails leading to the same place. The safety and autonomy of the species is best served by following diverse paths in small units.

Moreover, it is easier to conduct the affairs of small bands in which there is stronger bond. For a leader the task is then less onerous.

Furthermore, there is no contesting for leadership among the creatures. Leadership is a burden, not to be sought, but perhaps even to be avoided. A leader is chosen by consensus for his foresight to lead the way. He is, therefore, first in terms of showing the way and not in any other sense.

A story concerning a leadership contest illustrates what the Anishnabeg foresaw as the probable consequence of competition. According to the story, a loon challenged the crane for primacy among all the birds. The crane, unwilling to struggle to the death for such a burden that was both fickle and vain-glorious agreed as did other birds to surrender his primacy to the loon.

The loon assumed the position with pomp and considerable authority. The other birds, relieved to have someone willing to accept leadership, looked to the loon for guidance and for better life.

But it was not long before there was considerable discontent among the birds. By late August some birds were ready to leave for the south. Anxious, they called upon the loon to lead them. But loon was not ready, saying that it was too early and that other birds were not yet prepared to depart. The loon asked them to wait in patience. All would go. By the time the loon and all the other birds were ready to go, the sparrows and finches and robins had suffered considerable hardship, many having died by remaining too long.

When the loon and his massive assembly began their southward migrations, there were further complaints. In fact, there was dissension. Some complained about the speed of their flight; others muttered about the height of their passage; still more faulted the distances to be travelled daily.

On arrival in the south, there were other birds who had to go further south, but the loon refused to go on. In a hastily summoned conference, the birds called upon the loon to resign his leadership.

The malcontents, as the loon regarded them, argued, "You

have little concern for our differences or our needs. You are indifferent to our hardships."

Loon countered, "The well being of all comes first. I have to consider the general good."

The blue-bird retorted, "The general good has killed almost all of us."

Still the loon persevered, "I must think about all, not just one or a few."

The tanagers, black-birds, and warblers groaned, "You think too big. In thinking too big, you forgot the small." Without saying more, they left the loon as did the other birds.

Alone, the loon contemplated his presumption. The crane was once more accorded precedence.

Because the principles of leadership are best exemplified by birds, certain birds were chosen to symbolize leadership.

Leadership is a burden, uncertain for community and for the person to whom it is entrusted. It was to ensure, insofar as it was possible, excellence in leadership that the youth born of the totems symbolizing leadership were trained for their duties. In preparation, they studied history, tradition, grammar, and speaking. Part of the training fostered eloquence, wisdom, and generosity. It was hoped that such training would inculcate in the tentative candidate a special deference to the principle that in government the well being of people superseded all other considerations.

By custom, the elders invited a man of their choice and offered him the Pipe of Peace. Acceptance of the pipe signified acceptance of leadership, its smoking a solemn undertaking. The ceremony was often accompanied by the statement, "You have made me a poor man," because it was considered a hardship to lead, and because men were reluctant to accept the position of leadership.

But leadership was not always offered to those trained for it or to those born into the leadership totem. Merit was the criteria for assessing the quality of a candidate. Thus, if a person, born of another totemic group were deemed to possess a greater capacity for leadership than one so prepared, he would be preferred.

In the exercise of leadership, a leader did not act upon his own initiative. In matters that concerned the community he was expected to seek and rely upon the guidance of a council consisting of the leading men and women in the community. These were frequently the elders. In having the support of the leading people and in expressing their wishes, the chief would have greater authority than he might otherwise possess in the adjudication of wrongs, the settlement of disputes, the allocation of hunting and fishing territories, directing the movement of people to new hunting and fishing territories, or choosing between war and peace. While the composition of the council is not clear, it might be safe to assume that it consisted of the elders of each totemic group represented in a band. Again it is more likely that each community consisted of the five basic totemic groups.

Ideally, a man chosen to lead was a man devoted to the principles of peace, not war. But in practice, the selection of warriors as leaders could not always be avoided and there are numerous instances of war chiefs conducting the affairs of the community in a manner that was pacific. But it was always considered preferable to keep the civil leader and war leader separate. Their purposes were in conflict.

Accounts of leaders reflect the character and qualities expected of leaders. Kitche-Ojibway was a huge man, some six feet, eight inches in height, a warrior frequently on the war-path during which he had collected many honours entitling him to wear a head-dress.

On his return from one of his expeditions he found that his village had been attacked by the Dakota (Sioux) during his absence. Thoroughly inflamed, Kitche-Ojibway raised a war party consisting of twenty-two other warriors and himself. Against the advice of a medicine man whose guidance he had solicited, Kitche-Ojibway set out with his party to wreak vengeance upon the Dakota whose village was situated about three days walking distance toward the west.

Arriving in the vicinity of the Dakota encampment, Kitche-Ojibway's war party concealed itself in thickets about a mile from the village. They intended to attack the next morning. However, they were discovered quite by accident by some children and their dogs who wandered into the area. The frightened children raised the alarm: "Ojibway! Ojibway!" they screamed as they fled from the vicinity.

In a short while the village warriors, re-inforced by 150 warriors of two visiting bands about which Kitche-Ojibway did not know, rushed out to repulse the invading Ojibway. The startled Ojibway found themselves outnumbered. Nevertheless, they prepared to defend themselves honourably.

"Go home!" hissed Kitche-Ojibway to his warriors. Go home before it's too late."

"We have come too far to return now," protested the warriors as they prepared to defend themselves.

"Go home, quickly," commanded Kitche-Ojibway.

"We are not cowards. Our people would consider us cowardly, were we to run from the Dakota," the warriors countered.

"Go home," rasped Kitche-Ojibway as the yelling Dakota warriors drew nearer. "Go home," he repeated, "If you stay we will all die! No one will defend our village; there will be no one who will feed our families. Go while there is still time."

"But how shall we explain failure to avenge?" asked a warrior.

"You can take revenge another year, when you are stronger; when you are not outnumbered; when you have a chance. Go. I will stay."

At this last, the warriors stole away.

Kitche-Ojibway was never seen again, but he was not forgotten.

Such courage was not limited to men. Weegibance, Little Wood Fibre, was a grandmother and a member of the Leech Lake Ojibway bands.

The dread pestilence, smallpox, fell upon Weegibance's village. In a short while, the greater part of the villagers lay dead after hot fever and amidst excruciating agony. Weegibance filled ten canoes with the survivors, some of them already sick and all of them destined to die, in order to escape the place of death, and to avoid contaminating others. She led them on months of endless flight.

By day they paddled their canoes, always avoiding encampments of other people they encountered along the way; by night they camped without fires. All the while Weegibance fished and hunted to feed her people, gave them medicines to alleviate their sufferings, buried the dead. Although sick and believing that she would die like the rest, Weegibance struggled on.

One by one her friends and members of her family died, until only she remained. Resigned to death and too weak to go on, Weegibance prepared for her passing by putting into a small bay on an island where she collapsed on the beach.

When Weegibance gained consciousness, two men were sitting nearby cooking a meal and talking in muted tones. The old lady was horrified; she snapped at the men, "I am sick, I have the dreaded smallpox. "Go away." Then she began to sob.

"Then, it is too late for us," said one of the men in dismay. Nothing was said for a long time; Weegibance was too weak; the two men knew that they too would be afflicted. Weegibance fell unconscious again.

Later Weegibance awoke, the men were still there. They had not gone, but remained with her for several days bringing her broth made of herbs and feeding her. They did not get sick and Weegibance grew stronger.

After a week or so, certain that they would not become contaminated by the dread small-pox and confident that Weegibance had recovered, the men took the old woman home. One of the elderly men married Weegibance.

Labour

Among the Ojibway-speaking peoples, no occupation was more respected than that of hunting or fishing; that is, providing food; no men more honoured than the skilled hunter who kept family and community amply supplied with food and materials for clothing and shelter. Serving as totems of hunters were the marten, moose, deer, caribou, beaver, and muskrat.

Hunting demanded skill in tracking down game and patience in stalking moose and deer to get near enough the quarry to use a bow and arrow which had an effective range of about twenty-five yards. The occupation demanded endurance on the part of the hunter who often had to walk miles and even days if game was scarce and demanded strength to carry great weights. Moreover, hunting required resourcefulness in both summer and winter. To overcome and surmount the hazards and hardships represented by hunting was considered proof of individual worth.

That hunting and fishing were especially esteemed was publicly acknowledged in celebrating the first kill of a young boy. More often than not, it was the foremost hunter who was invited to be leader. In two ways, therefore, was the occupation of providing food given recognition.

The men and women so engaged satisfied man's basic and constant need. From the stories about Nanabush and other tales, one of the recurring themes was that of hunger and starvation reflecting fact and fear. Nanabush was constantly hungry. And it was not so much the scarcity of game as his ineptitude and anxiety that kept his larder empty and the bellies of his children emaciated. Had he skill and patience and resourcefulness, Nanabush might not have seemed quite so pathetic or bungling. But there were times when Nanabush was lucky in killing much game. On those rare occasions he and his family feasted to gluttony.

Out of the same theme of hunger and scarcity was born Weendigo, the glutton, the image of excess. The same theme produced legends of the disappearance of deer, roses, and the resultant hardships. Only hunters could alleviate hunger.

Compared to providing food, fighting was in the nature of a

dangerous diversion, to be undertaken in summer and suspended whenever the need for food superseded everything else. That Pontiac and other renowned war chiefs were able to assemble and retain a large number of warriors is testimony to the strength and force of their personalities and characters. But neither the urgency of war to protect land and freedom, nor even the magnetism of Pontiac could prevent the warriors from abandoning the cause to go home to feed their families.

The community and the families looked to the hunter to provide necessities and perhaps even a better life — where there was no hunger and where there could be laughter. From the woman's point of view, it was the skilled hunter who made the ideal companion in life. Their parents encouraged girls to choose well. In many communities it was customary to invite a young man to live in his future wife's household and to support her family for a given period as a test of his ability as a provider. It was not the warrior but the hunter to whom the community looked for a better life.

For a career in hunting and fishing training was long and arduous for every boy. It superseded all other occupations. Not only had young men and boys to learn about the character and nature of animals, but they had to learn how to make and repair their own equipment so they could survive in a variety of circumstances when alone. The young man became more independent and more resourceful; and as he became more resourceful, the better it was for his community.

The animal beings who symbolized the qualities needed for success in the provision of food were selected to represent those engaged in hunting and fishing and trapping.

The Defenders

Animals of fierce disposition, the bear, wolf, and lynx, were the totems of warriors. Warriors were a necessary evil. Directly and indirectly they caused fighting. For the most part, it was the youth who sought to be courageous; and, though there were several ways of so doing, there was no easier or finer way than through physical combat. Battle was a test for heart, strength, and skill.

There was little that the elders could do to prevent young men from going out to seek battle; they counselled against it knowing full well the consequences of such enterprise. Yet they were unable to stop young men from precipitating fights just as they could not stop young men from growing up.

The fights young men engaged in were not intended to end in the killing of anyone although this frequently resulted. It was sufficient for a young warrior to show his courage, put himself in danger, and overpower his antagonist. Fights were brief and often bloody, resulting in broken bones, heads, defeat, and wounded dignity. No matter the outcome of a mêlée, the spirit of vengeance was born that grew into enmity. Thus was fighting provoked.

Warriors instigated bad feeling and fighting; still, they were necessary to defend family and community from attacks.

It was desirable but not always possible to exclude war chiefs from the government of a community. In times of danger, the leadership of the community was entrusted to a war leader for the duration of the crisis. With the passing of danger the war chief was required to surrender his leadership role.

During crisis the war chief had only limited authority and power, proportionate to the number of warriors who followed him. Even then he had little control over his own men and probably less among the other members of his community whom he could neither compel nor constrain. His position was tenuous.

Any man could be unofficially war chief. Such office was not restricted to members of the Bear, Wolf or Lynx totems. It appears that the only qualification was courage, as demonstrated by the number of honours and battles won and by the small number of casualties suffered. Defeats and too many casualties lost for the war chief his influence and his following.

Any warrior could be war chief and raise a war party. As evidence of the limitations of his position, the war chief had to invite warriors to take part in his intended expedition by offering them a war pipe to smoke. A man, by smoking the pipe indicated his willingness to take part and formed a firm commitment from which there was no withdrawal. A man was also free to refuse the invitation; and since refusal was his prerogative there was no censure or recrimination.

In battle the war chief's authority was equally uncertain. No matter how carefully he may have planned his battle, he was never sure that it would be carried out; even a simple requirement such as the sounding of a whistle to commence battle was chance. The war chief could only hope. Too often warriors could not or would not wait for the signal.

Nevertheless, there were times when the war leader was able to exact from his warriors, compliance to a request not to attack until the whistle had blown. But once the signal was given, it was every man for himself; individuality and chance took over.

To the individual, a fight was not a war; it was chance to

prove one's worth. Warriors did not look upon a fight in political or economic terms; they did not regard a fight as a means to annihilate or subjugate peoples or to occupy land. It was purely a dangerous way of gaining and showing courage. But warriors did produce distrust, long standing hatred, and in some instances, a series of bitter fights.

Yet no alternative for the exercise of courage suitable to young men was offered by those who counselled against war. Not even fear of reprisal and injury to innocent deterred youth.

But in the main, the Anishnabeg loved peace, the existence of the Pipe of Peace and the Smoking Ceremony is symbolic testimony of this love.

Teaching

Men and women have to know as they have to grow in spirit. This basic premise presupposes the existence of teachers and imposes upon them the duty of teaching. The well being and the continuity of a community require that the spirit be enlarged and passed on from generation to generation.

What had to be fostered was not merely skill but understanding; not merely knowledge but wisdom. There was duty on the part of the wise to impart their wisdom and a concomitant obligation on the part of the unlearned to learn.

In general learning was two-fold: one end of training was to prepare man or woman to serve his physical needs; the other, to enlarge his soul-spirit or inner being. For the first, adults imparted their skills and knowledge to the young; for the second, the elders passed on their wisdom. Both forms of training were given at the same time. By combining both forms of training and teaching the product would be a well-rounded man, skilled and wise.

The end of one form of training was the development of skill; the other, preparation for the vision and fidelity to the vision once obtained, and ultimately the acquisition of some wisdom.

It was the elders, grandmothers and grandfathers who taught about life through stories, parables, fables, allegories, songs, chants, and dances. They were the ones who had lived long enough and had had a path to follow, and were deemed to possess the qualities for teaching — wisdom, knowledge, patience and generosity.

And if the stories that have come down to us are to be examined, they will be found to be simple yet complex. They are simple in the sense that they appeal to the very young; complex in terms of the scope and depth and number of themes in each. There is another element to the stories besides that of diverse themes and understandings — humour. That stories are humorous reflects the skill of the story-teller and the element of comedy in all aspects of life and living. A story well told should have at least four levels of meaning: enjoyment, moral teaching, philosophic, and metaphysical.

To foster individuality and self-growth children and youth were encouraged to draw their own inferences from the stories. No attempt was made to impose upon them views. The learner learned according to his capacity, intellectually and physically. Some learned quickly and broadly; others more slowly and with narrower scope. Each according to his gifts.

But when the time came, testings were severe. It was the only way in which a person came to know his worth and demonstrate his merit. He willingly submitted to the test of battle as he endured the long vigils of vision quest. A medicine man or woman suffered long periods of training to seek knowledge. A hunter had to prove that he was capable.

The more resourceful a man, the more whole he was, and the better for his community. The community had a duty to train its members as individuals not so much for its own benefit though there was that end, to be sure, but for the good of the person. The man or woman so trained had received a gift from the community which he was to acknowledge in some form; and that form consisted simply of enlarging one's own scope to the fullest of his capacity. The stronger the man, the stronger the community; and it was equally true that the stronger the community, the firmer its members.

To represent the noble vocation of teaching the fishes were chosen as emblems. Fishes are hidden behind rocks, live unseen in the dark depths, but remain steadfast in the swirling current.

What training was given was rendered in roughly three stages. During the first seven years of a child's life, the women and the elders looked after and taught the children. In the second stage, young boys went with the men to learn hunting and fishing while the girls remained with their mothers and the elders. The third stage began when a person started to seek wisdom from others.

It was during this last phase in life that the learner realized his want of knowledge, and sought out the wise to teach him. A man or woman begins to learn, when he seeks out knowledge and wisdom; wisdom will not seek him. He may never attain it, but he can live by those principles given to him.

Healing

For medicine men and women, the first symbols were the otter and the turtle.

However, birth into either the otter or turtle totems did not ensure a person a career as medicine man or woman. Healing was not a sinecure for persons of particular birth. The sole standard was special gift.

Because healing was unique and special, not dependent solely upon knowledge of plants and their curative properties, but upon a singular personal curative power, boys and girls deemed to possess this faculty were chosen by medicine men and women for training.

Once chosen, the candidates underwent a long period of apprenticeship under the tutelage and guidance of a medicine man. The training was designed to enhance and enlarge that curative faculty and to confer knowledge of medicines.

Initially, healers were herbalists. But as knowledge of medicines increased, there was a need to perpetuate and disseminate the knowledge. From need, associations were formed to spread and share new knowledge and understandings. Eventually, the herbalists became medicine men; and the medicine men became philosophers concerned not only with preserving life and mitigating pain, but also with offering guidance and principles for living the good life whose end was to secure general well being.

They reasoned, and by so doing, brought another element into medicine, that the well being of the body was directly related to the well being of the inner being of a person. Sickness, at least certain forms were construed as the physical form of inner turmoil. Consequently, the healing of an ailment included, in addition to herbs, inquiry into the nature and character of dreams.

Even in this development, some medicine men and women remained herbalists; others became herbalist-philosophers.

As thinkers, the healers established the Midewewin and set up the code of right conduct, or the code for upright living. Adherence to the code was voluntary. But medicine men and women who wished to influence others had to observe the provisions of the code. At the same time abiding by the code, it was believed, would bring greater curative powers under the premise that good fosters greater good.

From the healers came ethics which had application not only to themselves, but also to others. Healing, therefore, went beyond the sick; it applied to the well equally. It applied to the individual and from him to the community. More than this, it

71

bordered upon metaphysics, psychology, ethics, morality, and ceremony. It touched upon the training and education of persons.

For the knowledge that medicine men possessed, there was fear; for his healing, respect. Few men and women were endowed with the spirit for healing and preserving life.

TOTEM EQUALS BROTHERHOOD

The bonds that united the Ojibway-speaking peoples were the totems. The feeling and sense of oneness among people who occupied a vast territory was based not on political considerations or national aspirations or economic advantages; not even upon religion or similarity of view or ceremony; but upon the totemic symbols which made those born under the signs one in function, birth, and purpose.

It was through the totems that brotherhood and sisterhood were engendered. Speakers all commenced their speeches with, "My brothers, My sisters." In this manner was the bond that existed given formal sanction and expression. Such was the closeness of the bond considered that marriage between man and woman of the same totem was prohibited.

Men and women were considered brothers in purpose and duty. Leaders were, under these terms, brothers in function; warriors regarded one another as brothers, as did hunters and teachers and medicine men. Men engaged in similar callings were brothers and looked upon one another as such.

Although united by bond of totemic relationships, similar in outlook and understanding, speaking one common language, and observing one tradition, the Anishnabeg were diverse and autonomous. Perhaps distances may have precluded political and economic unity, but the sense of independence and individual freedom was, it is suggested, too deeply entrenched in the Anishnabeg character to encourage submission to a central government, adherence to one set of laws as required by political and economic union. Nor did they feel that one community ought to submerge its well being or commit its destiny to another.

The individual must be free; so also his community. By having its own leaders, controlling the conduct of its own affairs, following customs of its own devisement, each community was free. No community dared presume to interfere with the affairs of another, even in war. In all matters, a community was free.

There was among the Ojibway-speaking peoples one language, a similarity of understanding, but no union; what held the people together was the totemic system. Men and women belonging to the same totem, regarded one another as brothers and sisters having obligations to each other.

Duty

The Anishnabeg were, like other peoples, concerned about duties. What did a man owe to his community? What to his neighbour? What to his family? What to self? What forms of duty was he required to discharge? When? To what extent? What was the nature of duty? Were there natural duties from which there was no release? Does a promise exact a duty of fulfilment similar to that which arises from natural laws? To these questions, there was no final answer except further questions raised in stories.

Zhawano-Geezhig (Blue or Southern Sky) sensed that he would die from certain injuries that he had suffered accidentally while hunting. One night as his young family, consisting of his son, Cheebik (Root); daughter, Kayaushkonse (Little Seagull); an infant son, Myeengun ("He who makes strange noise" now commonly known as wolf) were seated near his pallet he said to his wife: "I will be gone soon. Look after the children." Turning to his sons and daughter he gasped, "Look after your mother. Be good to her." Amidst tears and sobs the children nodded. And within a few days that winter Zhawano-Geezhig died.

The spring of that year, the Mother, Weengushk (Sweet Grass) took sick. Daily she grew worse, eventually spitting blood. Knowing that she too, like her husband, would die, Weengushk spoke to her son who was about sixteen years of age. "Look after your sister and your little brother."

"Yes, Mother," murmured Cheebik.

The dying Weengushk extracted a similar promise from her daughter. Like her brother, Kayaushkonse solemnly undertook to look after her brothers.

Weengushk died leaving her two eldest children to look after Myeengun, an infant of two.

For a while the family of sister and brother lived quite amiably. But about two years after the death of their parents, Cheebik began staying away from home sometimes for days. At first, Kayaushkonse said nothing about these absences. However, when they interfered with the provision of food, she protested. Usually following her complaints Cheebik would improve, then would forget and neglect his brother and sister. It seemed that matters only got worse.

One day after a particularly severe reprimand, Cheebik reluctantly and somewhat ashamedly confessed that he had fallen in love and intended to marry.

Hearing her brother's intentions, Kayaushkonse was dismayed and shocked. She angrily reminded her brother of his promise, "Don't you remember your promise to mother? Are you now going to break your promise and abandon us?"

To this accusation Cheebik had no reply except, "You and our little brother can live with us. I have told the woman I'm going to marry about us. She is willing to look after all of us."

Cheebik was interrupted by his sister who screamed at him between sobs, "You care more for a stranger than for us. You care more about yourself than for your mother. Go. Leave us alone. I will keep my promise; I will not break mine. Go!" As she finished, Kayaushkonse pushed her brother violently out the doorway.

Cheebik was gone. Somehow Kayaushkonse managed to feed herself and her little brother for the next three or four years. There were desperate times, but they survived.

One evening Kayaushkonse was cooking a meal when a young man emerged from the forest. Since she had lived all her life in a remote area and had seldom seen young men, she was frightened; she, therefore, said nothing. Seeing that the girl was alarmed, the young man explained that he had been out hunting and was returning to his village without having encountered any game. Kayaushkonse fed the young man saying that she didn't have much to offer him. After the young man, Meegwun (Feather) had eaten, he thanked Kayaushkonse and then left.

A few days later Meegwun returned, gave Kayaushkonse some venison which she cooked. But he did not remain. The next day, the young man came back with more food. Thereafter, Meegwun came regularly every few days to bring meats and fishes of all kinds.

Gradually, Kayaushkonse overcame her bashfulness and began to talk to Meegwun telling him about her parents, her brother, her promise, and her circumstances. Meegwun replied that he had heard about them.

As Meegwun's visits became even more frequent and equally pleasant, Kayaushkonse realized that she was falling in love. It was pleasant, yet not entirely welcome. Against her stronger sentiments, she attempted to discourage him by saying to him one day, "You mustn't come again."

Meegwun was hurt, but he declared to the girl, "I love you. I want you as my wife."

"I cannot. Not now. I must look after my little brother as I promised my mother. He comes first," said Kayaushkonse.

"We can look after your brother; you can still live up to your promise," replied Meegwun.

74

"Much as I have come to love you, I cannot betray that promise. Can you not wait?" Kayaushkonse almost pleaded.

Meegwun was not easily dissuaded.

"You have an obligation to yourself too. You owe yourself a life. But your brother has no corresponding duty. When he is old enough to leave, he will leave. Where will you be then? What then?" asked Meegwun.

Kayaushkonse could not get Meegwun out of her mind, nor his words. For several days, she sat disconsolately in her lodge to be interrupted occasionally by her little brother who asked, "Why are you sad?"

Alternately, Kayaushkonse resented and pitied him, taking her brother in her arms or turning her back to him.

Early one morning, while her brother was still sleeping, Kayaushkonse gathered up her belongings and skipped out of the lodge.

The next day she and Meegwun came back to the lodge to get her brother. To their dismay and horror, the boy was gone. They scoured the nearby forest, Myeengun had vanished.

Days of search followed, but were fruitless. Sadly Kayaushkonse and Meegwun gave up their search. Nevertheless, they came back from time to time more out of duty than out of any hope of finding the child. Kayaushkonse desponded.

Some six or seven years elapsed before Meegwun returned alone to the area where Myeengun had disappeared. He was stalking a deer when he heard someone call out his wife's name, "Kayaushkonse." Meegwun froze in his tracks. Its voice was clear and querulous, "Kayaushkonse." Meegwun knew the voice of Myeengun. He too called, "Myeengun" and his voice echoed through the forest. Then Meegwun heard the mournful howl that sent icy chills down his spine "Ooooooo."

Meegwun edged over a small knoll. There in front of him sat a dark grey creature resembling a dog, but larger, his head pointing skyward all the while howling dismally and sadly. Meegwun rose, and as he did so, startled the animal who glanced at him before making off.

Meegwun knew that he had heard and seen Myeengun, "He who makes strange." He did not tell his wife about it. But he told his people and his children about Myeengun, the wolf, the creature who does not trust man, but runs. Meegwun used to say, "When you hear a wolf howl, remember that he is warning his brothers and sisters of the presence of man and to beware."

The story of the eagles reveals another aspect of the concept of duty.

"Tomorrow we leave," announced the father eagle to his sons and daughters. Autumn was not far off; it was almost time to leave for the south.

"Stay here and rest while I go out hunting." So saying the great eagle flew off and was soon out of sight. But it was hard for the young eaglets to contain their excitement at the prospect of going south to a land they had never seen, but had heard so much about. Consequently, they chattered noisily and flitted here and there in restlessness. Their mother unable to restrain, reproached them without much success.

Around noon, the great mother eagle scoured the skies for the return of her mate and somewhat worried, dispatched her eldest son to look for his father.

"Go and look for your father. He should have been back by now." The eldest son needed little encouragement. He soared into the heavens.

When neither father nor eldest son returned after an hour the mother eagle now more alarmed, but concealing it, sent two other young sons to search for the missing.

Like their brother before them, the two eaglets gladly shot into the air in different directions.

A little later the mother, now restive, sent two more out with instructions to scour the bushes in the valley below. But this time, the mother eagle was thoroughly frightened; and the eaglets remained famished. She tried not to show her agitation so as not to alarm the youngest.

One by one the eaglets returned to the nest as the afternoon wore on. They were by then all alarmed. As the sun waned and the shadows grew long, the eldest son returned covered with perspiration and breathless.

"Mother," he gasped, "I found father some miles from here, entangled in a tree, unable to fly. He has broken a wing."

"Come," the mother eagle screamed as she bolted into the air. Almost as one, the eaglets streaked into the clouds, silent except for the thundering of their wings. In a short while, they dove downwards to the glade far below indicated by the eldest brother who was leading the way.

When they arrived, the mother eagle and her eldest son as quietly as they could, lifted the stricken helpless male from his entrapment among the limbs of tamarack entwined with vines. They placed him on the bare branch of the tree. Unsteadily, the great bird perched there with pain instead of fire in his eyes, his great wings drooping down, weak and limp and useless, at his side. In vain, the mother eagle wiped the blood from the wing of her mate and snuggled up against him. There was no relief, and the pain made the great eagle totter uncertainly upon his perch, wheezing and gasping for breath. The young looked on helplessly.

As best as she could the mother eagle tried to bring some comfort and relief and solace to her mate. But she knew as he did that from this hurt there was no recovery, not even time and nature would heal the fracture. There was only slow, painful dying.

Whispering in agonized effort, the great eagle said to his mate and children, "You must leave tomorrow as planned."

Before he could say anything else, the young eaglets almost as one interrupted their father protesting, "We will not go without you. We will wait, no matter how long."

The old eagle rasped, "You must go, all of you. I will join you, when I am better. Your mother will lead the way."

At the mention of her name, the female eagle denied that she would leave, "I will remain with you. I am your companion for life."

The old eagle shook his head sadly, "No, you must go. You must look after the children, they need you."

Looking into her mate's face, the female firmly repeated, "I will not leave. I will tell our children how to get to the south. Our eldest son will lead them. They are old enough and strong enough to look after themselves."

So saying, she called her eldest son to her side and instructed him on to the direction of flight, the distance to cover each day, the height to traverse, the foods to eat, what dangers to avoid, and when to return. Finished, she assured her son, "Father and I will join you when he is well again."

Early the next day the eaglets reluctantly took leave of their parents and vaulted into the skies bound for the south, miles and days distant.

The great male eagle teetered on his perch though he clasped the branch of the tree as tightly as his ebbing strength would permit. His wing hung limply at his side; the feathers once glossy and firm were now dull and frayed. His eyes were misty and dim and his beak drooped. His voice cracked. No more was he a being and spirit of grace, power and beauty. He was an image of abject dissolution as he swayed upon his perch.

Best as she could the female brought food to her mate, shielded him with her body from the winds and the rain, flew up into the skies to repel the vultures who waited for the end, or flashed to the ground to repulse the wolverines and lynxes who gazed up hungrily. But for the most part the female remained close by the side of her doomed companion.

From his side, she sensed him growing weaker. Even though he pleaded with her, "Leave before it is too late," the female eagle kept her vigil.

The first snow fell one morning. Turning to his mate the great male, now dishevelled and emaciated, scarcely able to maintain his perch complained, "It is so hot. Will you wipe my brow?"

As he said so, he lost his balance, weakly flapped his one good wing before plunging from one branch to another, like some broken lifeless piece of skin, and fell in a heap upon the place below. With a cry the anguished female flew down to the lifeless form of her companion, uttering cries of despondency and lamentations.

The following spring, the eaglets, now grown, returned to their birth-place to seek out their father and mother, but all they found were a few soiled and tattered feathers underneath the tree where they had once parted.

INAENDAUGWUT — IT IS PERMITTED

Regarding the universal question of "what is man as a man entitled to," the Anishnabeg would probably have replied, food, clothing, shelter, personal inner growth, and freedom. To all other matters respecting man's relationship to other men and women and to society in general they would have said, "inaendaugwut," it is permitted: or "inaendaugozi," he is permitted of himself. Such term was predicated of many aspects of life, living, and relationships: it was a mode of understanding and interpretation.

Events were permitted by forces outside of man himself; the exercise of personal talents and prerogatives permitted by men.

Before Kitche-Ojibway the renowned warrior undertook his fateful war expedition against the Dakota, he consulted a wise man as to the fortuitousness of his enterprise. The medicine man advised Kitche-Ojibway not to embark upon his plan. Against the advice the warrior chief proceeded with his venture which ended in his death. It was said of the expedition and the result, "it was not permitted."

Just as a war leader had no control over the outcome of a battle, neither had he much authority or control over his warriors. By custom he asked and invited warriors to join his expedition. The warriors invited could either refuse or accept. A sufficient number of warriors subscribing to the war party to ensure success was a form of permission; too few accepting was a mode of denying permission.

A civil leader had certain prerogatives which he exercised not constantly or permanently but only on certain occasions and only under certain circumstances. He was permitted.

One of the prerogatives of a leader was to speak, but when speaking he did not purport or even presume to speak on behalf of his people without first seeking their guidance and their opinions upon the matters to be discussed. By deferring to custom and the will of the people the spokesman was seeking permission. The people on the other hand in granting permission were deferring to the speaker's eloquence. Finally, the willingness of an assembly to listen permitted a speaker to speak.

There were further limitations on the matter of speech quite apart from public speaking. The Anishnabeg related speech to credibility.

Daebaudjimod, the great raconteur and man who knew about everything, gradually and eventually lost the confidence of his listeners. Though men and women continued to listen to him, they did not believe his accounts. Listeners used to say of poor Daebaudjimod, "He knows too much, no man can possibly know as much." Some even said that "he talked too much." And the doubts continued even when events vindicated Daebaudjimod. The freedom to speak is related directly to scope and credibility.

The notion that matters were permitted, that a person was permitted of himself governed many aspects of a man's relationship vis-a-vis another and with his society and community.

The Anishnabeg's society was based upon what he considered to be his basic rights; his relationships upon the preservation of his personal freedom to grow in soul-spirit and in accordance with the world.

The Midewewin

THE MEDICINE MAN, WOMAN

The Anishnabeg prospered in the early years on their island home. Then a deadly disease descended, and threatened to wipe them out. Every person who became sick died; no one recovered. One of the victims was a boy. Asked by the Watcher whom he met at the entrance to the Land of Souls, why he was sorrowful, the boy replied, "Because the people are dying."

The Watcher delivered the message to Kitche Manitou.

Kitche Manitou, pitying the Anishnabeg, promised to send Nanabush to them with the gift of medicine. And he restored the boy to the Land of the Living.

Sometime after the boy's restoration, Nanabush appeared among the afflicted Anishnabeg. He sought out the young man who had been restored to the Land of the Living. Believing that this young man possessed the mystery of life and well being, Nanabush determined to teach him the art of healing.

When he found the young man, now called Odaemin (strawberry or heart berry), Nanabush took him to a secluded glen. There they prayed for guidance and for vision. As they wished, Nanabush received a vision. He saw an otter, pale and weak with sickness, bearing a branch in his mouth. The animal stumbled his way to a lake, swam out, and then appeared to be engulfed in the waves. The lake became quiet. When the otter emerged a short while later, still carrying the branch, he appeared to be stronger. He was cured.

Nanabush, happy, awoke from his sleep. He roused Odaemin. Taking the young man into the forest, Nanabush dug into the soil and withdrew the Kenebigo-wushk (snake root). In gratitude for his vision and the gift that it had brought, Nanabush constructed an open air lodge and said a prayer of thanksgiving within its walls. He prepared medicine from the roots and administered it to all the men, women, and children who were ravaged by the disease. Soon, all recovered.

During the next few years Nanabush taught young Odaemin. Plants, he said, possessed two powers, the power to heal and the power to grow. Nanabush, moreover, taught young Odaemin that plant beings could lend their powers of healing and growing to other beings. Animal beings possessed this knowledge. Odaemin must learn from them. The greatest lesson that Nanabush imparted to Odaemin was how to learn.

Nanabush left; Odaemin continued to learn. Daily he watched animal and plant beings. He observed what plants, roots, and leaves the bears ate; what the deer; what the beaver; what the partridge and the eagle. He watched what animal beings took when ill or wounded. Odaemin learned what root and plant made the moose well; what the wolf; what the owl. By watching the animals, Odaemin learned the properties of plants. What knowledge he gained, the mode of learning he used, Odaemin passed on to the Anishnabeg.

Odaemin found that the power to heal was not a gift bestowed upon every person. Even for the person endowed with this unique power, it was still necessary for him to foster the power and increase it. The gift had the capacity to confer growth and well being. What was required was not only knowledge of plant and self, but also the capacity to conjoin and make one the curative elements of both plant being and human being. Only a person endowed with and fostering the inner curative power could receive the inner curative power of the plant and confer his own upon the plant.

From Nanabush, and from his own experience, Odaemin learned that sickness would never be effaced from life. It was a state of being and existence, as abiding as well being.

Sickness and disease with their concomitant pain, being constant, the knowledge of medicine and the power to heal were to be perpetuated. If the ravages of disease were to be mitigated, then Odaemin, the first medicine man, was to teach others and pass on his knowledge.

Medicine and its practice was to be kept alive. Moreover, the gift of medicine was to be acknowledged in the celebration of the Midewewin.

To keep alive the wisdom of curing, Odaemin chose a young man endowed with special gifts, to be his student. The training was long, arduous, and intense. Only when Odaemin died, did the young man succeed.

Such was the way medicine men and women received their training; the mode and form of training became custom.

The inner being in which the gift to heal reposed, had to be enlarged.

During the early years of his training, a young man or woman chosen for his special gifts, spent time in meditation and prayer. Alone in a secluded place, the young person sought a dream. At the same time he endeavoured to impart his being to the plant and animal beings as he attempted to ingest their inner substances and make them part of himself.

In these retreats the medicine man or woman, it was hoped, would come to know himself and attain a high order of curative powers. Such retreats continued throughout the career of the medicine man. As the earth annually renews itself, so the medicine man had, each year, to withdraw into himself in order to maintain his powers.

Training was long and difficult and study continued throughout life. Only with the death of the sponsoring and practising medicine man or woman, did the understudy succeed. Not until then could he conduct his own affairs.

While he prepared his inner being and his character for the exercise of the gift, the medicine man studied plant beings. As he came to know the nature and the mode of existence of plant beings, the medicine man correlated his time and mode of collecting and gathering the life giving plant beings.

Roots were taken in the spring, when they were soft and replete with the fluids of life. It was then that the roots possessed the greatest forces of life giving substance. As the root was lifted from its cradle of soil, the medicine man intoned a prayer:

Your fibre is soft
Your fluid rich
Let us make the weak
Well and strong.

After the root was taken out, tobacco was offered to the four cardinal points, to Father Sun, and then placed in the bosom of Mother Earth.

Leaves, buds, and stems were collected in the late summer after they had fulfilled their first purpose of lending beauty to Mother Earth. They were then ready to serve another purpose.

In picking, a prayer was said:

Your spirit
My spirit
May they unite to make

One spirit in healing.
OR
You have given beauty
Now give the gift of well being.

Every plant had a place and purpose; every plant had a time. For every plant being there was a prayer and song.

THE MIDEWEWIN

As medicine men and women studied the nature of plants from the conduct of animal beings, they amassed a wealth of knowledge. Both necessity and desire to know more induced them to come together in association.

They came to realize that long life was not to be attained by a knowledge of medicine and healing. Healing was not a perfect art. Medicine men and women found that men and women still fell ill and died before living out their full terms of life. Something more was needed; some element was missing. To the medicine men, illness was a misfortune that represented punishment. They reasoned that the full life was not to be procured by knowledge of cure, but by living a good life. In their meetings the medicine people considered that which constituted a good life.

There was, they remembered, Kitche Manitou's command to commemorate and perpetuate the gift of the knowledge of medicine in and through a ceremony. To celebrate the command was an act of fulfilment of a pledge to the creator undertaken by Odaemin. Wherever the Anishnabeg established their villages and homes, they too commemorated the gift of knowledge annually in ritual.

In this way another dimension was added to the art of curing and the career of the medicine man.

Committed to the belief that long life was the product of good, upright living, the medicine men and women had to discover what constituted integrity in life, and having found it, live it out.

In his life the medicine person declared his integrity to the plant beings and to the world. Praying to the plant, the medicine man pledged that the power of the plant was to be used only for good.

Medicine men had not only to appear to be upright; they had to be upright.

Since good sprang from the heart and since men and women were engaged in conferring good upon their brothers and sisters, their celebration of the gift of medicine was known as the

Midewewin. The term is probably a contraction of the word "Mino" (good) and "daewaewin" (hearted). The word may also mean "the sound" or "sounding." Drums were sounded in the ceremony to summon the spirit of well being; rattles were shaken to dispel the spirit of suffering and ill health.

In the beginning, admission to the Midewewin required only knowledge of plants and the power of healing. With the introduction of morality into medicine practice, members were required to possess good character. For men, the receipt of a vision was a further requisite; there was no comparable requirement for women. Integrity of life and conduct was essential for both. Thereafter admission into the Midewewin was by invitation only.

Men and women added to the Midewewin character and strength by possessing integrity. In turn they received strength and substance from the Midewewin.

At the same time they gave form to the ceremony of admission and confirmation in the membership of the Midewewin.

No person could apply for membership in the medicine society; instead, the society invited men and women of good character into the fraternity. The invitation was extended only after long assessment of the character of the candidate.

It was customary for a member to propose the name of a candidate to his colleagues for invitation. The sponsor would then ask three members to visit the candidate for a feast which was followed by examination. After the feast, the sacred pipe was smoked (the tobacco supplied by the candidate). Then the sponsoring medicine man and his colleagues examined the nominee. They questioned him about his dreams, his life, and his vision. The examining body assessed the merit of the man, based on the quality and character of his accounts. If they deemed him unsuitable for invitation, they withdrew from the lodge; but if they deemed him meritorious, the examining members discussed the offerings to be collected and rendered; then they assigned a tutor to him.

In all, there were four orders through which the candidate must pass before he gained accreditation (but there have been instances in which a member went through eight orders before attaining full membership). Moreover, there were minor variations in different areas of the land of the Anishnabeg. The ceremony, however, was substantially the same in all cases.

The First Order (or Degree)

For a year the candidate received instructions from the tutor assigned to him. Once or twice a week he went to his tutor and mastered a body of knowledge, learned the names of the plants, their uses, character, quality, and the songs and prayers to be rendered to each. The candidate had to assemble the offerings to be given at the Midewewin to be held in the spring.

Many days before the invitation ceremony the candidate, his sponsor, and his tutor sent out invitations to the members of the Midewewin to attend the ceremony. All persons invited received a small bundle of splints to be discarded at the rate of one daily, so that each man and woman so invited knew the day of the ceremony.

Five days before the initiation ceremony the candidate arrived at the village where the initiation rites were to take place. On arriving he constructed his lodge apart from the main encampment.

Over the next four days, the candidate fasted and prayed to prepare his incorporeal self. Each day he cleansed his body in the purification lodge. In this way he presented himself to the Midewewin clean of heart, mind, and body.

On the morning of the initiation ceremony, the candidate remained in his lodge until summoned by his sponsor, who conducted him to the Midewigun (the lodge).

The Midewigun, in which the ceremony was to be conducted, was in form like the lodge that Nanabush first constructed.

Around the central Midewigun was an enclosure whose purpose is to keep the spirit of the celebration.

The Midewigun itself was rectangular, oriented east to west, an entrance at each end. The lodge was open at the top, free to receive life, light, and the sound of the whole world and the universe.

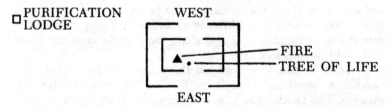

Within the lodge stood a cedar post, cut alive, and erected as the tree of life. Known as the Midewatik, it represented the world of the plant beings. At its base were placed the offerings of the candidate, which he had assembled during his period of preparation.

Near the Midewatik was a fire, the symbol of one of the four basic elements of the world.

From his lodge the candidate was conducted by his sponsor and tutor to the Midewigun. At the entrance to the outer enclosure, they were met by four bears, emblematic of all that is good in life. In the four circuits around the central Midewigun, the initiate and his sponsor would be escorted by the four bears, who would remind and encourage the candidate as he made his symbolic way around the sacred lodge. Four other bears met the entourage. Representing evils and temptations that the candidate would encounter in the moral order, these bears obstructed and impeded the way.

That the candidate would meet temptations in his life and career was depicted on the holy birch bark scrolls as a path with nine digressions and sometimes seven paths leading from life's main trail.

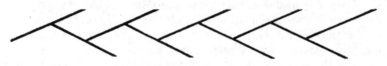

According to the Midewewin, to digress from the true path and not return was tantamount to death. But digression was often only transitory, seldom permanent. It was for this reason that the members of the Midewewin were expected to retreat annually in vigil and in prayer, to ask for guidance. During the retreat the medicine man reviewed his life to determine whether he was on the true path. Of temptations and evils, man was reminded by the hindering bears; of digressions and capacity for renewal, the candidate was reminded in the sacred scrolls.

There are four stages in life; infancy, youth, adulthood, and old age. Four times the candidate, his tutor, sponsor and escorts proceeded around the Midewigun before gaining admittance into the inner sanctum. On and along the way he must not falter and yield to forces of evil.

When, at last, he completed the fourth and last circuit, the candidate presented himself at the eastern entrance for admission. The candidate's admission into the Midewigun may be regarded as a symbol of the triumph of good over evil.

Admitted and welcomed into the central lodge, the candidate entered into a new mode of existence and a world of becoming.

He chanted:

I come
Trembling,

Weak and unlearned
Teach me!

The assembled members, sitting in rows facing the candidate chanted in response:

Behold
A new brother
Let us welcome
Our new brother.

After the songs the sacred pipe was lit, and passed around.

At the motion of the presiding and senior Midewewinini (Medicine Man), the candidate sat down for testing and examination. He had to answer all questions and demonstrate that he had mastered all the knowledge that he had been assigned. There could be no mistakes.

Then the presiding Midewewinini or Midewequae (man or woman) shot the candidate with the Midemegis (a shell). The candidate fell dead, unmoving. The Midewewinini revived him with the breath of life, as Odaemin the first medicine man regained life. The candidate stood, renewed, and new.

Such was the dramatic way in which the state of non-existence and resurrection were demonstrated. The candidate now was not what he was before, but transformed. He had been reborn.

The sacred Midemegis represented and commemorated an event in the history of the Anishnabeg.

According to accounts, a large group of Anishnabeg left their homeland in search of the Land of Abundance. Thinking that such a land lay to the east, the band travelled for many years in the direction of the morning. They at last came to a great ocean whose waters were salt. Unable to go further, the Anishnabeg settled on the lands of the salt waters. So long did they remain that the men and women forgot their origin.

One day a small sea shell emerged from the waves of the great sea and hovered over the land of the Anishnabeg where it remained for a long time. It frightened the men, women and children; puzzled the wise and learned medicine men.

The medicine men and women went into seclusion and kept vigil until one of the elders received a dream. He dreamed of a land to the west, where the sun sank. The vision of the setting sun was to him as beautiful as that of the dawn.

When he related his dream to his colleagues, they interpreted his vision as a sign to return to their homeland which all, except the very ancient had forgotten. The elders remembered a previous land and existence only in story.

The medicine people told the leaders the meaning of the sea shell. And the leaders immediately commanded the Anishnabeg to dismantle their lodges and prepare to go on a long journey.

When canoes, paddles, bows and arrows were ready, the Anishnabeg began their homeward journey to the west.

One legend relates that the little sea shell floated in the sky always to the westward drawing the Anishnabeg ever back to their homes. Another story says that the little sea shell appeared and hovered in the western sky only when the Anishnabeg tarried too long in one place or strayed from the true path.

Led ever westward by the sea shell, the prodigal Anishnabeg after many months at last arrived in their own land. Some say that the Anishnabeg settled at Boweting (Sault Ste. Marie); others said that the Anishnabeg went further west establishing their homes at Moningwaukauning (now La Pointe in Wisconsin).

To commemorate this event in the history of the Anishnabeg, the men and women of the Midewewin used the Midemegis in the first three initiation ceremonies of the Midewewin; the little shell symbolized the return to the true path to find fulfilment and to resume purpose.

By rising from the dead the candidate demonstrated a power; it was also an evidence of the power of the medicine men and of the Midewewin. The initiate gave up a former way and a previous life and in rising up, assumed a new. The Midewewin took away one life and mode, conferred something not possessed before.

The initiate now demonstrated his other powers to the assembled medicine men and women. He then received from the presiding medicine man, the Midewiyaun (medicine bundle) in which he encased objects that symbolized his personal powers received, powers to be fostered to further growth. The medicine bundle was the outward tangible and visible image of the personal mystery of the new man, the new Midewewinini or Midewequae. Such was the personal nature of the Midewiyaun that at death, it was buried with the deceased as a mark of the termination of the substance of the man.

For the great gifts and powers received, a new existence, a new life, greater in scope and depth, there must be acknowledgement. What had been received was intangible; what the new member gave may only be represented by the tangible.

At this point in the ceremony, the candidate distributed the offerings that he had assembled during the year in preparation for the initiation. He gave his gifts to his new brothers.

One other ritual remained, before the ceremony ended. The history of the Anishnabeg was told. Recounted by a story-teller, he reminded the new member and the others of the path of life of a people and the gifts received from the grandfathers and grandmothers.

When the history telling was finished, the Midewatik (cedar post) was taken down and the candidate was conducted out of the Midewigun by the western exit.

The candidate was now a member of the first order of the Midewewin. As such he was entitled to paint a bar across his face. As an accredited medicine man of the first order, he could conduct funeral ceremonies and preside at Feasts of the Dead.

At the end of the ceremony or later, the new member could declare his intent to proceed to the next order the next spring.

Second Order (or Degree)

As before, the candidate who wanted to proceed to the next order of the Midewewin must prepare. A new tutor-sponsor was selected. Once a week the candidate for the second order received instructions from his tutor. And for a year, the candidate had to assemble gifts to be presented as offering; and master songs, chants, rituals, and knowledge assigned to him.

The Midewigun in form and structure resembled the sacred lodge for the first order ceremony. There was one difference; another post stood within the lodge.

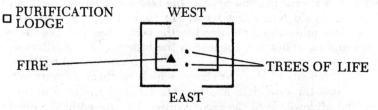

The candidate must remain in his lodge to await the coming of his tutor and escorts. All the while he chanted his petition to Kitche Manitou and to the spirit of the world:

My eyes are shut
My ears are closed
Open my eyes
Open my ears.

In the Midewigun, the little drums began to beat softly.

With their sounding, the tutor left the Midewigun to get the candidate. On behalf of the members, the tutor invited the candidate to the lodge. Slowly, accompanied by the four bears, he conducted the candidate toward the lodge. At the entrance to the outer enclosure, they were met by a snake, the symbol of evil and temptation.

Four times around the Midewigun, the candidate and his escorts were required to walk. All the while, the drums sounded within the Midewigun; the four good bears sounded the rattles to drive off the snake.

At the entrance of the Midewigun, the tutor and his candidate met the presiding fourth order Midewewinini. The four bears left; the snake disappeared. The candidate once more chanted his petition.

The attending members chanted their welcome and invitation:

> Let our brother's
> Eyes open, and
> Ears unblock.

To the sound of chants, and drums, and rattles the candidate with his tutor, made eight circuits around the interior of the Midewigun. He was then invited to sit down facing his examiners, eight in number.

There followed a test of knowledge and character and a demonstration of powers. Immediately afterward the candidate distributed his offerings to the members of the Midewewin.

He could now see far, even beyond the scope of sight; he could now hear matters beyond the range of hearing. Good and evil he could touch and sense. He could range far and wide.

One other ritual remained in the ceremony. The new member and his colleagues listened to the history of the Anishnabeg. They were not to forget the past; they must remember the accomplishments of their forebears and keep them in perpetuity.

Now the candidate had become a fully accredited member of the Midewewin of the second order. He was entitled to wear two stripes across his face.

The new member left by the western door.

Third Order (or Degree)

If the second order member of the Midewewin intended to proceed to the third order, he had to inform all members of the Midewewin of his intent. He was obliged to find another tutor to prepare his mind and spirit for testing and entry into the next order. In the period prior to the next initiation ceremony the candidate for the third order gathered presents for the offering.

In form, order and procedure, the ceremony for the third order initiation was much the same as the order and form observed in the first two orders.

For the third order, the Midewigun had three posts in the interior.

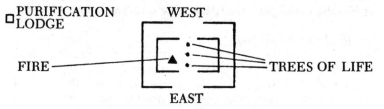

The tutor went for the candidate and brought him into the enclosure to the accompaniment of chants and drum and rattle soundings. With four bears the tutor and the candidate journeyed four times around the Midewigun. Four great lynxes who guarded the lodge, tried to discourage the candidate.

Entering the inner lodge by the eastern entrance the candidate petitioned in chant:

> I come
> From life old,
> I seek
> Life new.

The members of the Midewewin chanted:

> From another time
> Comes one.
> Into a new time
> Becomes a brother.

There was examination, the shooting with the Midemegis, the death. There was the expulsion of the Midemegis and the subsequent revival.

Restored to life, the candidate possessed powers not before possessed. That for which he prepared a year and petitioned in chant was his.

With his added powers, the third degree (order) member could become a Jeesekeewinini, able to summon supernatural powers and beings, cause vibrations in things for the well being of the afflicted, commune with the supranatural order and beings. As Jeesekeewinini, the member of the third order, had as his special patron the thunders. The power of the Jeesekeewinini was of the skies, the reason why he can move and shake things such as lodges. Added to his powers was the ability to extract hidden things and meanings.

When the ceremony was completed, the new member of the third order might, on special occasions, shade the upper portion of his face, green; the lower, red. For the Midewewin, green symbolized the south, the source of rains, thunders and regeneration; the red, west, the abode of shadows and death.

Fourth Order (or Degree)

The preparation for entry into the fourth order and last Midewewin was no different from those of the first three.

But the Midiwigun for the fourth order had three purification lodges on each side, and four posts in the inner sanctum.

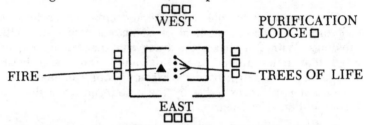

In his passage around the outer walls of the Midewigun, accompanied by his tutor and the forces of good, the candidate encountered the spirits of malevolence who, not only protected the integrity of the Midewewin, but also endeavoured to tempt the candidate. The guardian bears armed with bows symbolically shoot the lynx, turtle, wolverine, fox, wolf, and bear. In triumph, they kill evil.

Inside the Midewigun and before the assembled members, the candidate intoned:

> I come
> To die.
> I come
> For life.

The members responded:

> It is easy to die
> It is hard to live.

Revived from symbolic death, but real in a moral sense, the new member now possessed the power of conferring and confirming a like power in others. He was entitled to test the powers of candidates.

92

The candidate with his powers confirmed was a fully accredited member of the Midewewin, known by the green hue spotted with red covering the left portion of his visage. The number of spots equalled the number of times killed and restored to life.

A Midewewinini confirmed as a fourth order member had submitted to four initiations; four times he has been purified; four times tested; four times lost his life; and four times regained it. As he left the Midewigun and the sacred posts were taken down, the medicine man or woman of the fourth order was whole and complete.

Though complete, the Midewewinini was obliged to attend one ceremony of the Midewewin once a year for a renewal of himself and of his power.

One phase of existence ended; another began. In the moral sense, the difficult way commenced. The medicine person must do good works; he must guide others; and, he must himself, espouse a good life.

Without himself being of upright character, the Midewewin member believed he could not attain or confer the long life. He could not be true to his undertakings.

For their own guidance and for that of others, the members of the Midewewin devised a code.

CODE FOR LONG LIFE AND WISDOM

Thank Kitche Manitou for all his gifts.

Honour the aged; in honouring them, you honour life and wisdom.

Honour life in all its forms; your own will be sustained.

Honour women; in honouring women, you honour the gift of life and love.

Honour promises; by keeping your word, you will be true.

Honour kindness; by sharing the gifts you will be kind.

Be peaceful; through peace, all will find the Great Peace.

Be courageous; through courage, all will grow in strength.

Be moderate in all things; watch, listen and consider; your deeds will be prudent.

The Path Without End

THE CYCLE AND PERPETUITY OF LIFE

In a beautiful remote valley lived Eshkebug (New Leaf) and his parents. So far was he from any village that he had never encountered humankind except for his parents, on his frequent hunting expeditions. Withal Eshkebug was content enough, the trees, flowers, birds, and animals providing him with the deep companionship of brothers. He lived in harmony with his world taking game enough only to allay hunger, remembering always a prayer of thanksgiving to the creature which had given its life for the well being of his family. With early manhood came restlessness, and Eshkebug, although he could not have explained his actions had he recognized them, began to roam farther and farther afield in his hunting.

One day, far from his home, Eshkebug chanced upon an open glade in the forest. This he scanned carefully with his hunter's eye from its pinebounded sides, to its softly grassed floor. There, in front of him, the short grasses had been worn away in a clearly defined track. Eshkebug was startled. What animal could have made such a path?

Kneeling down, Eshkebug examined the prints of small, delicate moccasined feet on the earth. He contained his excitement with difficulty, and followed the footprints, returning at length to his original starting point. He had traversed the glade left to right counter-clockwise, only to return. This path was a circle. Here was a Path Without End.

In the centre of the circle the short grasses and flowers and the earth itself had been pushed heavily down. Puzzled by the huge, shallow depression, Eshkebug tried to determine its cause. No animal wore moccasins nor had so many feet, and all

94

of different sizes! Yet it appeared that some huge beast slept repeatedly in the centre of the circular path. Eshkebug knew no animal of such a size — the very grandfather of all bears! He squatted and examined the prints again scratching his head in consternation.

A thin, haunting strain of music enveloped Eshkebug. Enchanted, he arose, looked around, and again the music pulsed, swelling and diminishing, closer than before. From the westward, high in the blue vault of the sky, came a star flash, a sparkle in the afternoon sun. Slowly a sky-craft moved downward, feather-like. It hovered in careful descent, drifting closer to the glade in which Eshkebug stood. Eshkebug, moved by curiosity, yet fearing that such a craft must have supernatural powers, hid himself in the bushes to watch as the ship, surrounded by ethereal music nestled in the flattened depression bounded by the circular path.

As the craft settled into its resting place like a giant clam shell, which it resembled, sun dappled its dully glowing sides with a pattern of leaves and pine needles. The music stopped. At the top was an opening which quivered to uprightness, revealing an opulent interior. A vagrant hint of joyous laughter curled around the startled Eshkebug.

From the ship stepped ten maidens, each more beautiful than the last. They played happily with a ball as iridescent as their craft, tossing it high amongst their group and catching it as it descended. The girls tiring of their game skipped lightly around the path in an intricate dance with the grace and suppleness of young deer. So enthralled was Eshkebug that he remained hidden as they sat in the grass chattering gaily and gathering flowers, which they wove into garlands for one another. At last, tired of their play, the maidens arose and stepped back into their ship.

Slowly the top closed, and the maidens sang the melody which had heralded their descent. The craft rocked, lifted, and began to drift upward into the lengthening shadows of early evening. It vanished into the heavens.

Eshkebug returned home with tales of the remarkable sky-craft and its cargo of young women, to mystify his parents, and awakened in his mother the remembrance of old stories told by her family. While Eshkebug slept soundly she watched the fire for a long time, but the complete memory eluded her, so that she retired with a vague sense of disquiet and something akin to foreboding.

Eshkebug returned to the clearing in the forest the following day. Again the craft descended. Again the maidens played the afternoon away in happy chatter and dance. Each of the girls was beautiful but it was to the youngest of the maidens that Eshkebug's eyes always returned. It was the youngest who moved him, who caused his heart to rise to his throat. Resolving to speak, to make his presence known, Eshkebug stood up and called out, stepping out into the open as he did so, his hands held open before him to show that he meant no harm.

The maidens screamed in terror and fled into their ship. Hastily they intoned their flight-song, which wafted the craft into the sky leaving Eshkebug alone in the clearing, which rang now with silence.

Disheartened and sad Eshkebug returned home and told his parents how the sky-women had fled his friendly advances. The youngest maiden, he disclosed, he loved, and wished to marry, if only he could speak to her.

His mother, seeing her son disturbed, spoke at length on the sky-people and their special powers not obtained by the earth-bound, for she had adduced from the stories of her people, now, after much effort and time remembered, what manner of beings her son had come upon in the forest glade.

Eshkebug, firm in his intention was not to be lightly discouraged.

His mother pointed out that a sky-woman would not be content on earth since return to her people, even for a visit would be impossible.

Eshkekbug was adamant. The youngest maiden stirred in him a love that would not be put aside.

Deeply troubled, his mother remarked that the sky-people were unaware of time as it existed for mortals. Indeed some said that they were immortal. Could Eshkebug be happy with a woman who did not age as he, himself grew old and infirm?

The future, concluded Eshkebug, was always uncertain. Perhaps he would not live to reach old age. He wished the woman for his wife now, not in some far distant future time that might never be.

At length his parents wished him well, vowing their help in whatever way they could give.

And so, heartened and comforted, Eshkebug returned to the secluded glade with apprehension, fearing the maidens would never return, but hoping that they found earthly activities so entrancing that they would forget their fright at his sudden appearance. No sky-craft descended. Eshkebug waited. Night came. Presently he slept.

As he slept, Eshkebug dreamed. From the forest stepped a handsome young buck, who approached Eshkebug without fear. They regarded one another. Suddenly, the stag shimmered as does the sand in the dazzling sun and a man dressed in the hides of deer after the manner of Eshkebug's people, stood against the green of the pines. In his hand he carried a belt fashioned of braided hides. Around him shone a radiance of blue light.

"Your heart is known to me Eshkebug," the young man said, "Since you have always been sincere in your concern for the deer people, never neglecting to beg our pardons when you took our lives in your need, we feel kindly disposed to you. Therefore, we, the deer people confer upon you the ability to change your shape as you will. Such a power is yours only as you find it necessary in your quest of the moon-maiden. Yes, Eshkebug, it is from Grandmother Moon that the craft first came. Use this power wisely, and know that the deer people favour you. We will help you as we are able. Here is the symbol of your medicine," and he pressed the belt into Eshkebug's hand.

Before Eshkebug had collected his wits the young man was once again a deer bounding into the thicket. When he awakened the belt was tied firmly around his waist.

During the days of waiting that followed, Eshkebug considered his new power. He kept his vigil patiently, and one sunny afternoon the sky-craft again rippled from the heavens in its descent, surrounded by the chant that had first attracted Eshkebug.

His heart quickened, and he ran to the rim of the path without end. There he touched his belt and willed himself to become a tree. Shortly there grew beside the path an inviting young pine. Eshkebug waved his deep green branches in delight, offering shade to unwary moon-maidens.

The sky-craft landed in the depression. Just as the merry laughing girls were about to disembark, the eldest cried out in alarm.

"Wait, Sisters! That tree was not here before!"

Again Eshkebug watched the craft depart. He was forlorn and disconsolate as he returned to his former shape.

Give up? Not Eshkebug! Had not the deer people promised their help? He fasted and prayed, seeking renewed hope and guidance. Soon the stag bounded from the forest, and with a hazy shimmer of light became the young man of Eshkebug's dream. Now his eyes shone with controlled good humour.

"Eshkebug, my poor friend, I had thought to help you find a wife. No matter. Women are ever changeable creatures whatever their origin. Perhaps you seek to woo the eldest; she is quick of eye at least, and beautiful as well. But it is the youngest, the most timid who has moved you. So be it. When they come again, (for they surely will. Do not doubt it.) become a fawn. I, myself will be the doe near you. What maiden can resist the appealing sight of a young and helpless one? What is more natural to a forest than deer who roam at will? Take heart, my friend. We will allay the suspicions of the eldest. You're sure? . . . I see that you are." With a smile he vanished.

As the emissary of the deer people foretold, after some weeks, the sky-craft once more slanted down from the afternoon sky. Even as the song of the maidens ceased, Eshkebug had changed himself into a fawn, and a doe stepped daintily from the forest to his side. The two allowed themselves only a look of recognition before beginning to crop the grass side by side, ever closer to the Path Without End.

The eldest sister scrutinized the forest carefully before alighting from the ship. She stood some moments on the ground testing the air with her nostrils, listening to the birds who sang undisturbed, seeking harm in every flower and butterfly. Finally, she called "Come Sisters. All is well." Swiftly the glade was full of their unrestrained laughter and play as the sisters reunited themselves with the earth. Seeing the doe and fawn who had ceased cropping the grass to watch the play, the maidens approached them quietly lest they be frightened. They stroked the animals admiring their beauty, and the complete absence of fear they exhibited. In the manner of women, they crooned over the little one, marvelling at his snowy spots and minute feet, feeding him buttercups, and singing softly to him.

When the youngest maiden knelt to stroke his velvet muzzle, Eshkebug willed himself to become human, and seized her, running toward the forest amid the startled cries of the sisters, who fled into the inviolable sanctuary of their sky-craft. All afternoon the craft lingered as the maidens waited, hoping their sister would escape the fearful creature that had captured her. But as twilight came, believing her dead, they sadly sang the song of flight, abandoning the earth which had suddenly erupted in violence and uncertainty. No more would they return.

The youngest maiden, having fainted from fright was being borne in Eshkebug's arms to his parent's lodge. Although he was elated at the final capture of his quarry, Eshkebug became anxious at the stillness of his burden. He stopped to look down at his beloved in the moonlight and saw her long lashes flutter, heard her murmur, and exultantly continued his journey to the lodge.

It was Eshkebug she first saw when she opened her eyes to the strangeness, from her stupor of terror. He stroked her silken hair with gentleness but she cowered at the shock of his touch. Presently, Eshkebug's mother bustled in, pushing aside her son, who in perplexity knew not how to approach his captive without causing her harm. In truth all his time had been given over to schemes for her capture, for he had not considered the manner in which he should comfort his strange prize. His mother knew. She enfolded the frightened girl in her arms, rocking her as one does to pacify a restless child. Soon the maiden had ceased shivering. Presently, she no longer flinched away from Eshkebug's touch. Having accepted food, she slept.

They named her Geezhigoquae, or Sky-Woman, for she had come from the sky. Treated with love and kindness by Eshkebug's parents, and wooed by Eshkebug himself, she soon overcame her shyness and became accustomed to their different ways. Soon she assumed a share of the woman's chores in the lodge like a dutiful daughter, and seemed content with her new situation.

Before winter set in Eshkebug and Geezhigoquae were married. The following year a son, whom they named Zhawano-geezhig (Blue Sky), was born to them. Eshkebug was extremely happy. Yet as he watched Geezhigoquae's eyes he saw them touched sometimes by an infinite sadness. When she perceived his glance she would smile softly, and the lingering unhappiness would clear away. Many times he asked her about this when she turned and mumbled in her sleep, or when she would stop in the middle of lifting food to her mouth and sit transfixed for a moment. She always assured him all was well. Geezhigoquae found Eshkebug to be the gentlest and best of husbands. She was proud that her spirit had reached out to him that day long ago in the forest. She was glad that he had chosen her to capture. Now she was content to be his wife.

Shortly after Zhawano-geezhig's birth, Eshkebug was awakened by her quiet sobbing. He reached out, held her close murmuring endearments but she would not be comforted for many hours. A dream bothered Geezhigoquae.

She saw her parents, now grown old, heard them call her to their side. They asked to see their new grandson so that they might welcome him properly. A pressing need commanded her to do as they bid, to show them once, just once before they died, their grandson Zhawano-geezhig. Each knew that this could not be.

Geezhigoquae held fast in Eshkebug's arms, mollified by his sympathetic presence, soon slept. But never did she forget.

As Zhawano-geezhig grew, so did his mother's longing to visit her parents become stronger. Eshkebug would have taken her on the journey if it had been possible, and his inability to accomplish this saddened him so that he tried harder to please her in all things.

If she could not return to the lodge of her parents to visit, perhaps Geezhigoquae would find comfort in a replica of the sky-ship which had brought her to him, thought Eshkebug. He could not duplicate the shining rainbow material that composed her former craft, but birch-bark used by his people to fashion canoes seemed an original substitute. When he unfolded his plan to her, Geezhigoquae's eyes gleamed with bittersweet remembrance and she smiled at him through a mist of tears. It was agreed that Eshkebug would gather the bark, and she, aided by Zhawano-geezhig would fashion a ship. Zhawano-geezhig, now grown straight and handsome and with the sunny disposition that comes to a well loved child was vastly excited by the prospect.

By autumn, the craft was complete; a small, round, shell-like structure lashed with cedar strips stood before Eshkebug's lodge. Geezhigoquae often sat in it with her sewing, remembering her youth as her fingers flew over her work. Her eyes looked back on that far away time as she told her attentive son the stories of her people. Zhawano-geezhig, fascinated by the sky-craft he had helped to produce, and his strange ancestors, often came to sit with her.

When curiosity prompted Zhawano-geezhig to ask how a woman of the moon came to meet and marry a man of earth, she laid aside her omnipresent work and spun the tale for him ending with her capture.

"My sisters fled to the ship in terror at the sudden appearance of your father," she said in conclusion. "We did not know what manner of creature pursued us endlessly, nor his purpose in the harassment. Indeed, I am happy that he sought me out, yet I still long to see your grandparents once more. Imagine their flight-song, and the sorrow in the lodge of my parents when they returned without me." She picked up her sewing and sighed.

"Mother, sing the flight-song for me," requested Zhawano-geezhig.

His mother laughed softly, "It is a woman's song, son," she said. "Still I will sing it for you, only if you promise never to repeat a note. Misfortune comes to men, even small ones, who sing the song of women. No sky-craft ever leaves the Moon without women to sing the song of flight.

Zhawano-geezhig was intrigued. "I promise, Mother," he vowed.

Geezhigoquae paused, remembering and began the song

that had brought her to the entranced Eshkebug. Again more strongly as memory returned, she chanted the melody. The craft quivered. Lost in her memories, and unaware that even in such a different ship she would still retain the power of flight, Geezhigoquae sang on. Zhawano-geezhig remained still in surprise as the ship lifted, floating above the trees and into the sky alighting on the Moon before the lodge of Geezhigoquae's parents.

What feasting there was that night for the two astonished travellers! Amid the song and dancing and laughter Eshkebug was forgotten.

But on Earth, in the lodge of Eshkebug, only sorrow was present. Arriving home after the hunt he had found the sky-craft gone, and knew its destination. What was a man to do? He knew his wife's strange origin, but such was his love that he felt the beautiful earth would compensate for the loss of her parents and her home. Eshkebug was sure that he had gained his wife's love. He believed he had made her happy.

Again, seeking guidance, mindful of former help, he fasted and meditated, until once more the mighty stag stepped from the woods to become a man surrounded by shimmering light. Here was Eshkebug's patron, he of the deer people. Compassion lit the face of the young man as he spoke briefly.

"Only wait, Eshkebug, wait. Perhaps you will wait forever. Wait. Hope. Do not give up." Then he was gone.

In the realm of the sky-people, Zhawano-geezhig remembered his father with longing. Excitement had filled his arrival. His grandparents were kind and indulgent. There were new places to explore, new games to play, but Zhawano-geezhig became melancholy. He missed his father.

"Let us go home, Mother," he begged.

"Soon," she replied.

Alas, time for the sky-people has little force and meaning. Only Zhawano-geezhig was aware because he was of the earth as well as the moon. He asked often. Always the answer was the same.

"Soon," she would reply. "Yes, soon, my son."

Zhawano-geezhig entreated his grandparents, "Send for my father."

Because the elders loved their grandchild, they agreed.

"Go," they said. "Bring your father back. Tell him we expect a gift of a bird of every kind. Take your mother's eldest sister as pilot for your craft, for she is wise and will help you." They embraced their tall grandson.

In the valley of his birth Zhawano-geezhig found his father, old now, and lonely. When the tale of Zhawano-geezhig's adventures had been told, and Eshkebug knew that Geezhigoquae had not deserted him with intention, but by accident, a great weight seemed to lift from Eshkebug's heart. Soon they had captured birds of every kind, filling the ship with a feathered rainbow.

Thus it was that Eshkebug came to the moon, and was re-united with his wife and son. A feast of welcome was prepared, at which he gave his father-in-law the birds he had commanded.

The birds, released, flew into the heavens to become a new group of stars. Swan-like they stay to remind us of old Eshkebug in his new home.

The Path of Souls
(of Death and Afterlife)

THE MILKY WAY

Geezhig (Cedar) and Wabun-anung (Morning Star) were to be married in the spring. Having proved himself a capable hunter and demonstrating that he could provide for Wabun-anung by supporting her family all that winter, Geezhig had received permission to marry her.

Theirs was the promise of spring in the enduring love they bore one another in their lives and in their living. Happily they contemplated their future together with mundane plans for happy years of beloved companionship and children from their union. But as the first new leaves of spring unfurled and the robins declared their promise of new life to come, Wabun-anung died. All promise died with her.

Geezhig gave himself up to grief. His eyes bright with tears he could not shed, he spent endless days gazing into the fire or wandered along paths he afterward could not remember. He hunted no more. Food remained uneaten since all nourishment choked him. At night, staring into the blackness his heart heavy in his chest, he remembered until he could bear the pain no longer. Summer came and with it a resolution grew within him. Wabun-anung had been taken from him. Surely she had no wish to go. He would, he must go to rescue his lost love from the Land of Souls.

Telling no one of his resolve, Geezhig took up his medicine bundle and his weapons, and approached his beloved parents. "I am going to find Wabun-anung," he declared.

Geezhig's father, knowing his son's grief, shook his head in sorrow, "She is dead, my son. Wabun-anung is dead. You cannot bring her back from the Land of the Dead."

103

"I must try Father."

"Geezhig, Geezhig," sobbed his mother, "Leave the dead alone."

"I cannot, Mother."

As he walked from the lodge through the early morning dew, they watched him, resignation and apprehension in their faces. When he disappeared into the forest, they sighed and took up living again wondering if he would survive the dangers of such a journey yet each knowing that in no other way would their son know the finality of Wabun-anung's death.

Geezhig's quest took him from village to village, from one wise man to another, from friends to strangers. Everywhere he asked the same question, "Where is the Land of the Souls?" Everywhere he told the same story. "She whom I was about to marry, has died. I am resolved to go to the Land of Souls and have her restored to me."

No one knew with certainty the direction Geezhig should take. Some said it lay to the south; others felt the way was west. Helpful they were and kind, but they were as ignorant as Geezhig in placing the Land of Souls.

All were bewildered by Geezhig's quest and his intensity of purpose. Men and women tried to assuage his sorrow as best they could.

"Geezhig," said one wise man, " it is not good to seek the unattainable. Give up the hopeless quest which can only bring more suffering to your burdened spirit. Rather, try to make your spirit peaceful, and composed so that when it is called into the Land of Souls, it will be tranquil and wish to stay. Burden your spirit in life and it will retain the memory of sorrow in the Land of Souls."

Good words and wise which neither diminished Geezhig's pain nor lessened his resolve. Geezhig continued his search.

"My boy, out of your loss you will know gain," wheezed an old grandmother, her back bent by the burdens of sorrow in life, whose heart had known many sufferings which cut as deeply as Geezhig's loss, but whose eyes remained bright with the joy of life. "It is better to have known and received love, however short, than never to have known it at all. Through your tragedy you will come to know life and be better able to give and receive love hereafter."

Unmoved, Geezhig went on.

"Destiny governs portions of our lives; it permits certain events; prevents others. Accept what has been apportioned to you knowing that perhaps you avoid an even greater calamity through the misfortune inflicted upon you."

104

Wise, sagacious, and true Geezhig realized. Nevertheless he went on.

Geezhig listened to another woman, her greying head shaking with the infirmity of the very old. "You are not the first, nor will you be the last, to endure adversity. We sorrow when good ends; we grieve when what ought to be comes to naught; we lament when beauty fades away. For every ending there is a new beginning. So it is in spring when the trees that shed their leaves in the autumn regain their foliage in season; a rose cut down springs up from its root. And so, when a man suffers adversity, in loss of love or loss of home, he must renew and rebuild on the ruins. Geezhig, begin again."

Solace was not to be found. Wisdom and commiseration could not restore his beloved Wabun-anung. For love's pain, healing does not come from others.

Up to this point Geezhig had been travelling in no set direction, wandering rather in search of knowledge. One night late in autumn he sat staring into the embers of his fire, thinking that, since there was no ease for his heart in indecision he would search for the "Path of Souls" about which he had heard much during the summer. Geezhig reasoned that in following this path it would lead him ultimately to the "Land of Souls" and Wabun-anung. He must travel neither south nor west, opinion as to direction had been divided, but attempt a south-westerly route midway between the points indicated. Then if he could not find the "Path of Souls" he could try west and south in turn until a better method presented itself or until he was called to the Land of Souls himself.

Geezhig travelled many months traversing numerous rivers, swamps and lakes. He went through country he had never heard about, met people whose languages and customs were strange. He ate little, slept infrequently. Dreams of Wabun-anung haunted him in sleep and wakefulness. Always, he went on.

In his quest he had encountered many paths, some well beaten, others obscure, before he came upon a path both wide and deep. A thick mist enshrouded the trees on either side and curled across the way to brush his cheek with a vagrant tendril. Within the bounding forest an occasional drop of moisture fell rustling to the leaves below. An owl hooted in the distance. The fog swirled around Geezhig engulfing him in a blankness which obscured his vision. He had reached the "Path of Souls."

Shadows whose features were hidden from him walked with him at a distance on the murky way, all bound at an unhurried pace ever to the west. Geezhig went with them into the thickening gloom.

Silence held the soul-spirits, for such they were, as they, unresisting following their destiny. Geezhig knew that he, an interloper, must not interrupt their final dream, since he did not, by right, belong, in their number. For him, this was a chosen path from which he could turn if he willed it to be so. That Geezhig was tolerated among the rest filled him with hope.

How long did he follow the quiet trail? Time had no meaning. Suddenly through the curling fog loomed the rising slope of a mighty ridge. One by one the shadows disappeared down the crest into the thicker mist at the bottom of the slope. He, too, was about to descend when an ancient and withered man accosted him.

The old man spoke. "You are Geezhig," he said. "I have been expecting you. I also know what you seek. I know your sorrow but I cannot permit you entrance. The Land of Souls is for the dead. You live. My Son, go back and live out your life. She whom you seek passed by, in peace, four days ago. Your time is not yet, Geezhig, but when it comes, know that you will find welcome."

Geezhig entreated, "I cannot live a life made shallow without Wabun-anung. Her place is by my side; mine with hers."

But the old man frowned, "Your soul-spirit is yet conjoined with your body. Only soul-spirits may freely enter the Land of Souls."

"Then kill me!" Geezhig's words echoed hollowly. "Let me die here. I have but a little way to go. With Wabun-anung I shall know happiness and peace. Old Man, I implore, kill me now."

A gentle smile lit the wrinkled face of the Watcher, "Ah, Geezhig, I have no power over life and death. I cannot do this thing you ask."

"Then let me see Wabun-anung once more. Bring her here or let me enter for a little while. Grant me my wish and I shall be content. In return I shall do whatever you ask of me. Then I shall return to the Land of Living." Geezhig's earnest plea came from the depths of his being.

The Watcher considered. He pondered and at last answered. "I will help you. In return, I demand nothing for myself — indeed my wants are few — only that you return to the Land of the Living in peace to live out your life as Destiny requires. Regard me, Geezhig. Consider and question. There is that which holds me in this place belonging neither to the Land of Souls or the Land of Living. Remember it well.

"It is easy to find a way across the river, which appears deep and wide to some, narrow and shallow as a stream to others. In sleep your spirit may cast aside your body, which I will tend here until you return again, and go with the spirits of the dead to the other side. An adamantine bond remains conjoining spirit and body which may be severed only by death itself. By this link you will return.

"My boy, I fear for you, yet I know your anguish. See that you do not let grief overcome your judgement. Stay not too long in the Land of Souls. Perhaps you will forget what you see and what you do in that place but the journey will leave a mark upon you that cannot be erased. May you find comfort to sustain you until your own time comes."

Even before the old man had finished his warning, Geezhig became drowsy and slumped to the earth. As his eyelids dropped he felt a mystic force lifting his spirit from its abode within the tissues and fibres of his body. When this supra-natural metamorphosis had run its course, Geezhig possessed a new mode of consciousness, existence, and being. As a spirit he re-entered the engulfing mist and descended the ridge. His emaciated body in the care of the Watcher, remained on the ridge's crest, where he dimly knew spiritless its heart still beat, its blood still flowed. Yet he seemed to possess a body with moccasined feet to walk and eyes to see. His arms still swung at his sides. His ears still perceived a ringing silence.

Emerging from his passage through the mist, Geezhig beheld a land much like the one he had left. Before him a broad expanse of turbulent water rushed on its mighty course. This was the promised river. For Geezhig, wide and difficult the passage.

On Geezhig went following the course of the river, until at last it became placid, shimmering in the sunlight. Across its depths lay the Land of Souls.

He could sense the being and essence of that world. Colours seemed more vivid and varied, as if he saw them through the eyes of childhood. A bird song floated to him on the breeze. How deep the forest on the other side. How dark and cool it appeared. But how could he cross the river.

Small wavelets slapped the shore through the reed beds, drawing Geezhig's attention downward to a canoe moored on the bank. Beside it lay a paddle. Each beckoned, inviting him.

As he guided his craft carefully through the reeds to open water beyond, he sensed that he was being watched. Geezhig lifted his eyes and found he travelled with others, all bound for their ultimate destination on the other side. Close by him paddled his beloved Wabung-anung. As their eyes met and gazes held, all the loneliness and search, all the sorrow and sadness were wiped out, eradicated as if they had never been. Love flowed between them even on the river.

Geezhig called to her, lifted his paddle in salutation, tried to steer his craft to her. Though she looked her love and happiness, she did not reply, she paddled steadily for the other side. Geezhig, also, could not alter his course, but, thankfulness filled him and he thought, "I will speak to her in the Land of Souls. I have found my love again."

As Geezhig drew near the farther side, the water which had been calm before, became violent, turbulent, full of eddies and huge, jutting rocks. Water spraying on his shoulders as he gave himself entirely to the task of safe passage. Many of his fellow travellers were overcome, but Wabun-anung paddled serenely ahead surrounded by gentle waters which aided her passage. What happened to those who floundered, Geezhig was unable to tell. In such waters it was impossible to stop and offer aid.

At last the bottom of his canoe scraped earth, gritting on the sand beneath. Geezhig jumped out pulling at his craft. Wabun-anung stopped beside him.

To Geezhig came the call.

"Now you have seen. Your wish has been fulfilled. Return to the Land of the Living."

Geezhig turned his canoe around and recrossed a river suddenly shrunken into a small steam, to the Land of the Living and life.

The Four Hills of Life

Weegwauss (Birch) awoke sweating and trembling from the midst of a dream which so disturbed him that he could not go back to sleep. He had to understand his dream. For the remainder of the night he pondered, but at dawn Weegwauss was no closer to a satisfactory interpretation. He got up, put on his clothes, and went out of his lodge to look for Chejauk (Crane), the wise man.

When he arrived at Chejauk's lodge, Weegwauss called out, "Chejauk! I must see you. I need your guidance."

"Come in," said Chejauk, yawning and stretching.

Weegwauss walked into the lodge and sat down.

"Why do you disturb my rest, Weegwauss?" said Chejauk. "What can be so important that you arise at dawn before the birds?"

'I have had a very strange dream. It disturbs me a great deal so much that I cannot go back to sleep. I must know what it means," said Weegwauss in agitation.

Chejauk indicated that Weegwauss should sit and then stirred up the fire. He filled his pipe and lit it before inviting, "Tell me your dream."

Weegwauss began: "I was standing on a high hill overlooking a deep, wide, and enchanting valley. It was quite unlike any valley I had ever seen and I gazed upon it, captivated. After a long time I turned my gaze from the valley to the other side. Across this vast expanse I saw four great hills. The first was steep and jagged; the second and third were less steep and rugged; the fourth was craggy and almost perpendicular, the top enshrouded by a thick white mist. And even though the hills were distant, I saw them clearly and everything upon them.

"On the slope of the first hill were countless infants crawling from bottom to the crown. At the base, only the smallest, youngest, and frailest were to be seen. As the infants proceeded toward the crest they got older and stronger. Near the top were the oldest infants. Of the vast number who began the ascent, only half, it seems, reached the top. Some scarcely began the journey before they slumped to the ground and lay still. Others continued a little further before they collapsed to move no more; still others, stronger and sturdier struggled on, but they too were stricken and breathed no more. Happily, some survived, attained the crest and descended the other side of the hill. I was among that crowd of infants. I saw myself survive the hardships of that first hill.

"I next looked upon the second hill. How different; yet, how similar. Here those who had been infants on the first hill were now young boys and girls, bigger, stronger, and sturdier; some appeared to be quite well on in years. Others were hardly seven or eight.

"Unlike the quiet nature of those on the first hill, the boys and girls on the second hill were full of energy. They could do many things. They had greater scope, greater powers; they played games of racing, wrestling, swimming shooting; they worked, carrying wood, picking berries, hunting, and fishing. Laughter filled the hillside. But just as often as the youths were happy, they were grave. In moods and abilities and scope those on the second hill had greater range than those on the first.

"In other respects the scene was very much like that which took place on the first hill. There was the same compelling irresistable motion toward the top of the hill. There were the same calamities on that vast wide road. Boys and girls perished along the way; some in their play; some in their work; others in sleep. They drowned in streams and lakes; a few had violent choking; some were slain by human shadows. There was life; there was motion; there was death; there was no stopping.

"Seldom did the survivors stop to help the stricken. When they did pause, it was to remain only for a few moments and hurry on again. None turned back. They seemed unconcerned about the sick and the dying and the injured; it was as if they cared only for themselves. Something, a force, an object, a purpose drew them ever forward toward the summit of the hill. When they reached the crest they hurried down the fatal slope. I, too, hurried with them. Ahead was the third hill.

"There seemed to be little difference between the third and second hills. Some of the faces that I have seen on the first and second hills appeared among the crowd of climbers. There was the same unflagging, constant and forward pace. There was the

110

same loss of life and unremitting reduction in numbers. There was the same indifference to the dying by the living.

"But how different all else; how changed. There were, on the third hill, no infants or youths to be seen, few games to be witnessed, little laughter to be heard. Men and women began to travel in pairs, although there were solitary travellers, both men and women. All, paired or alone, were bent upon reaching the top. Little else mattered; pleasures were few and short lived.

"Men worked at various tasks, hunting, fishing, making and repairing tools and instruments; women laboured by a fireplace cooking; or in a lodge making and mending clothing; blending medicines.

"In between the tasks and the infrequent joys, there were shouts of anger and hatred. There were battles between peoples over matters of little importance. Too frequently quarrels ended in pain, injury, and death.

"On and on the masses marched with unperturbed pace. Two by two, one by one the marchers stumbled and slumped to the ground to rise no more. But no calamity, no impediment, no pleasure halted that surge of human beings. There was no pause, no rest, no turning or looking back. There was only one motion, forward.

"At the peak, the marchers and I among them, who had survived, shouted in triumph. The goal so difficult was attained. The descent looked easy but was fraught with dangers and perils. Men and women fell, got up, stumbled, gasped, and lay still forever; women sat down to rest and sleep, never to wake again. The way down was as treacherous as was the way up.

"Above the wayfarers towered the fourth hill. How few we were; how old; how creased and wrinkled; how white of hair; how frail. It seemed impossible that these feeble and broken bodies could scale or even attempt to crawl the jagged rocks of the heights.

"Still we went on. Had we not overcome the first and second hills? Had we not conquered the third mountain? Why not the fourth hill? With faltering steps, halting strengths, gasping breaths the decrepit struggled on. Some inner strength of spirit urged us on; some outer force pushed or enticed us onward, forward, upward.

"But neither inner strength nor external force was enough to carry us all to our distant goals. Old men and ancient women crumbled to the ground and were engulfed into the mountain soil to become one with it. Those living on looked back, shouted encouragement to the fallen, to the faint. They shouted even to those on the third hill.

"On we went, undaunted by the loss of companions or life partners, undismayed by the ordeal, anxious to reach the misted crest. Most succumbed on the incline. Few reached the summit. But I was one of those who did not collapse. I lived on. I struggled on. Those of us who continued to live slowly vanished into the shroud that hid the crest.

"At this point I woke up. I do not know whether the dream is good or evil. I come to you for guidance." Weegwauss waited for Chejauk to answer.

The medicine man spoke calmly without looking up. "It was a good dream, Weegwauss. You saw life from beginning to end. You saw man's life in its entirety, in all its stages, in all its moods, and in all its forms. Kitche Manitou, the Great Spirit, has been generous to you. He has allowed you to see all of life in dream. He grants this privilege to only a few. As you saw life, whole, continuous, and uninterrupted, so will you live out your own life to its very end. You will see your grandchildren and your great grandchildren. You will suffer sickness and enjoy good health; you will endure adversity and know prosperity; you will encounter both good and evil. You will survive, while others will never reach the fourth and final hill. You need not fear that death will cut off your life before you have lived it out in its entirety and before you have served your brothers."

Chejauk refilled his pipe and lit it carefully. At length he puffed a cloud of aromatic smoke and continued.

"As I understand it; man's full term of life extends over four stages: from infancy to youth and then to adulthood terminating in old age. Few men or women live to see old age. Many never get beyond the first stage, infancy; many more never go further than the second stage, youth; those who outlive the first two stages, attain the third, adulthood, may never know the fourth, old age. Life is too difficult. There are too many dangers, disasters, and perils along life's path. For men and women to live out life in all its stages is to receive and possess nature's greatest gift. As hills are difficult to overcome so these stages in the course of human existence are sometimes called hills.

"The first hill that you saw was the first stage in the life of mankind, infancy. Many children are born. They are small, frail, helpless. All they possess is potential, nothing more. They are without personality and character. Yet they bring happiness and hope to all, parents and grandparents and strangers.

"You say that you saw many babies die. So it is in life, which is sad. Few, in relation to the number born, live on. The coughing sickness chokes the life out of them before they have begun to be; it kills them even before they can begin to understand how to know. I think death for them is easy, but death does come, easy or difficult. Who can say about another's passing? Nor should we regard their passing as final. Perhaps, they will be born again in forms new and different; perhaps, their spirits will return to infuse new beings. This is the hope that sustains all of us.

"Death is always tragic. That all people are destined for death from birth does not mitigate the grief of passing for those who love the one who dies. But the death of infants is doubly tragic. They, so helpless, unfulfilled, and dependent, cannot be protected by those stronger. The wonderful promise is cut off before it can begin to be fulfilled. Anticipated beauty, happiness, and goodness are crushed in their very budding. What ought to be comes to nothing. A light flashes and is swiftly extinguished before it begins to illuminate. After the flash it is dark again. Death comes too soon or too suddenly severs hope for men and women.

"For parents, not only is the promise stricken, but their very act of love, their blood, their extension is negated by death. The joy of motherhood is too soon crushed and all too brief after prolonged distress of child bearing and long anticipation. The gladness of fatherhood is but momentary. Both suffer from helplessness in the face of illness. They are powerless.

"Those surmounting the first hill and reaching the base of the second in safety, must go to the next. There is no pause, no time for celebration. The journey must continue. Such is life; such is the great law that prescribes one continuous journey.

"The second hill is that of youth. It is a time in life when the young begin to bloom in spirit and flourish in physical power and stature. What is striking is that youth encompasses many ages. There are those very young, hardly out of infancy; there are those who are much older. But no one proceeds to the next stage until he has received a vision. Until that time, a man or woman remains a youth.

"As youth consists of many ages, it is composed of many qualities. Among the young will be found the gifted and the mediocre, the strong and the weak. But no matter their worth, all must meet and overcome the tests along the way.

"Continuing from the first stage, the physical struggle for simple survival goes on. Sicknesses cut down strong and weak alike even before they are well on their way up the hill. Sometimes it leaves others to continue a little way up before striking them down. It leaves some lame, some blind, some deaf; others, it renders frail. Others remain whole and unscarred. The shadows you saw attacking some travellers were enemies and murderers.

113

"Nothing can stay death or injury. Neither the skill of medicine men nor the healing power of herbs have force enough to prevent a killing or repair mortal wounds. No wisdom can negate the agonies along the way. Youth itself is no bar to pain, hardship, and death. Still, the struggle goes forward. The urge to live exists in strong and frail.

"In this phase the young begin to learn the arts, the skills that will enable them to conduct the life struggle alone. Boys learn to hunt, fish, make their own equipment, and to fight in defence of families and homes; girls master cooking, sewing, teaching, and looking after the well being of others. Only through enduring effort are these skills acquired.

"At the same time youths receive another kind of training intended to prepare them for a different form of struggle. It is two-fold in order, physical and moral. On the physical level the training makes the flesh ready for physical endurance and for the reception of the vision. It is believed that the great vision would not come until both the earthly frame and the spirit are ready by test and worth. There are, therefore, two great ends in training: to render a person capable of looking at his physical needs; and to discover his nature, essence, and purpose through a vision.

"It is said and believed, 'that no man begins to be, until he has seen his vision.' Before this event, life is without purpose; life is shallow and empty; actions having no purpose have no meaning. Consequently, youth is a time of preparation for the coming and reception of the vision.

"From the moment a youth begins to understand, his training and preparation begins and continues until the vision comes to him. Between the ages of twelve and fourteen he ought to begin to seek his vision. Because no one knows when the state of readiness of body and spirit is attained, the teaching and preparation continues. In some cases the state of fitness comes readily and early, in other instances, much later in life. But the teaching and instruction end only at the vision.

"For youth, the struggle in the moral order consists of the preparation, seeking, and attainment of the vision. What makes the search difficult is that the vision is not to be sought outside of oneself: nor is it to be found outside of one's being. Rather it must be sought within one's inner substance and found therein. Since it will be found within a person's inner self, the search must be conducted alone, without the assistance or guidance of others. There are no signs to mark the trail; there are no trails set by others to encourage the seeker. The object is unknown, the message to be received profound. It may be clear or obscure;

it may be pleasing or displeasing to the seeker. But it must be sought whatever its nature, and it must be accepted.

"In and through vision a person may see, hear, sense, or even feel his first self, his incorporeal substance. By vision he will discover that his nature demands growth in order to attain fullness and power. From the moment of the enlightenment the seeker has a purpose. From the moment of the coming the seeker is obliged to regulate his deeds according to the vision. In a way a vision is discovery of self and what ought to be. Growth begins.

"Whether the vision coincides with the aspirations of the seeker or is contrary, the vision seeker must understand the essence and nature of the vision. Moreover, he must accept its dictates and live by them. If the vision is suitable, the easier it is to accept. There remains the matter of living it out and giving expression to it in daily life. If, on the other hand, the vision is not what was expected, changes have to be made in order to live out the vision. It must be obeyed. The vision, whether favourable or adverse, must be understood and then lived out.

"While the vision gives an insight into the quality of the inner being, what it is and what it ought to be, it can do no more than give some direction about the course of life. Nevertheless, by some force the vision can change a man, give his actions meaning, lend purpose to his intent and growth to his spirit. After receiving the vision, the seeker must follow the principles given to him.

"With the vision, existence becomes living; the youth is no longer young. He has now a freedom which only he and no other can exercise and fulfil. It is his own. Yet his freedom and independence must be consistent with his communities' laws and codes and with the great laws that govern the world. Through vision a person goes from youth to adulthood.

"In character the third hill is less steep and less rugged than the first two. It is not less difficult to climb. The burdens and duties of parenthood must be discharged. The weight and uncertainties of leadership must be born by men and women. There are battles to be fought; disputes to be resolved; and, provisions to be obtained. Men and women must tend the ailing and look after the infants, youth, and the aged as they must care for themselves. In form and scope and variety, the third hill is the most formidable of all.

"But in the number of those who fail along the way there is no difference between the third hill and the others. Men and women falter from their burdens at the foot of the hill. As they continue to climb, more men and women are crushed by disease and war. Even approaching the summit, more human beings stumble never to advance or come nearer the goal. Ever and ever the number of walkers diminishes, more die. Few are the survivors.

"While men and women contend with the struggles in the physical order, they must live out their visions. They must follow the path of life as is prescribed in the visions. In so doing they must observe the laws of the world and the customs of the community. At times, laws, customs, and codes may appear to bridle and restrain the vision and bind the freedom of the individual. But the conflict is only apparent. General world laws and codes and customs are wide enough to allow a person sufficient scope for the exercise of his freedoms and for his growth.

"Nor is this the only impediment. There is the sanctity of the vision and persons of other men and women. Duty requires that persons honour and respect the individual spirit and vision of others. And the most suitable, and the least objectionable way of exercising this respect is by allowing others to exercise their growth and scope, by non-interference. At the same time a man or woman must not allow another to interfere with his vision. The vision must remain inviolate. And for it to retain integrity, it must not be surrendered to others in any manner or for any reason. To give a portion of it, even for a brief time, is to yield a portion of the spirit which leads eventually to loss of freedom and harm to the vision. For the same reason no man or woman ought to attempt to seek the control of another's vision and person. Visions must be kept whole and unimpaired if freedom is to be retained and growth continued.

"But the chief difficulty in living out the vision comes not from outside but from within a person. It is hard to follow the path of life in conformity with the world and in concord with other men. Much more difficult is it to live by the hard principles of the vision within one's self. The heart may go against the mind; reason may resist feeling; expedience may be contrary to need; chance may interfere with the order of things; codes may thwart the sense of justice; unforseen forces may act and nullify the vision.

"When such forces move, they may make men and women do things they ought not to do; they may induce men and women to neglect that which ought to be done; they may encourage men and women to prefer the easy to the difficult; they may persuade men and women to do last things first. The hardship in living out the vision comes from human frailty, and want of understanding; not from evil or malice.

"Men and women ought to remain on the true path set for

them. But human experience tells us that such is not always possible. For all their good intentions and endeavours, men often lose their way.

Because men and women stray from the path of life, the way is shown as having seven branches on which the traveller is allowed to digress seven times. But he must return to the true path without impairing his vision seriously or without betraying his trust.

"Whenever a person loses his way, he must, of his own accord, find his way back. No one else can assist him. Only he knows the way; only he knows where and when he departed from the true path.

"Morally and physically the way up and the way down the third hill is tortuous. Men and women suffer and die physically; never do they complete their life's journey. Men and women abandon their vision never to attain fulfilment. But they live on and endure. Now they are very few.

"Adulthood ends. The mood of life and people alters. The pace of men and women and life changes. Even the tone of living varies. But though all else may change, the stuff and substance of life remains the same. Where adulthood ends, old age begins.

"There is continuity, there is no break.

"In the evening of life, the aged give way to decrepitude and must accept the loss of strength, the lessening of endurance, and the wane of agility as part of life's destiny and the consequence of continuing to live. A former way of life must be forsaken; a new mode of living accepted.

"But to give up the old and embrace something new has always been difficult. For labours, pursuits, habits, manners, and pleasures that have become part of a man or woman are not easily cast off. The more familiar and cherished former ways, the more difficult the parting. Though former modes can no longer be exercised, they live on in memory. By their very sweetness and worth they call out for living on; they deserve to be repeated in life again and again. What is good needs to be regenerated many times over.

"To resurrect the past in forms already done, is to negate survival. The same flower does not live, die, to live again. It lives, dies, and is no more. After death and passing it leaves a memory of loveliness and a promise of a renewal of that beauty in another flower in another spring. To resurrect former times and to relive them would end the fulfilment of visions and growth in the new order.

"Perhaps it is the knowledge that what was can never be again — can never be restored except in fresh modes that render old age most difficult. Men and women know that death is inevitable. No wish can defer it. Men and women are destined for it from birth. The end must be accepted as part of life.

"When men and women attain the last weary hill and climb toward the crest, they are sustained by the knowledge that they have lived out their visions and given a helping hand to their fellow beings. Old age is a gift of the Kitche Manitou. As such it is to be cherished; not disparaged.

"Even in old age, life's work is not finished. There is still much good that can be done for brothers in life. By living through all the stages and living out the visions, men and women know something of human nature and living and life. What they have come to know and abide by is wisdom. This is what they must pass on to those still to traverse the path of life and scale the mighty hills. Only when they finally vanish into the mists is the work over."

Chejauk concluded by saying, "I have given to you what I have understood. There is more, but my mind cannot compass the depth and scope of the thoughts of wise men on the subject of life. I leave it to you to grasp it in your own way, in your own time, and according to the powers of your mind and heart. Think on it. You are indeed fortunate to have had such a dream."

Chejauk said no more. Weegwauss got up, said, "Farewell. Your words are wise," and disappeared into the light of a new day.

The Vision
(Self Understanding and Fulfilment)

"No Man Begins to be Until He Has Seen His Vision"

"No man begins to be until he has received his vision" perhaps best expresses the Anishnabegs' fundamental understanding of man's purpose in life and by distinguishing between living and being posits the existence of a moral order. In turn, this basic understanding is predicated upon the concept of the essence and nature of a human being.

According to the Anishnabeg, man was a spontaneous being made out of nothing; that is, created from new substances unlike those out of which the physical world was made. Out of corporeal and incorporeal substances was man created according to and in fulfilment of a vision of Kitche Manitou. Man was, in the abstract metaphysical sense, a composite being.

But as the Anishnabeg conceived man as a being endowed with a capacity for vision much like his creator, man became more than an abstract being, a creature of the mind. Man was bound to seek and fulfil vision and as such was a moral being. His life therefore was to be regarded in a moral sense.

Men were required to seek vision; moreover, they had to live out and give expression to their visions — it was through vision that a man found purpose and meaning to life and to his being.

There was another aspect to the nature of man. In scope and depth and breadth, every man was very different; some were gifted; others possessed lesser powers. Still each was obligated to seek in his own capacity, his purpose not outside himself, but within his innermost being. And because each man was differently endowed, every man attained a different vision; each fulfilled his vision as he and not someone else understood it.

For the Anishnabe the vision became the theme and quest in his life that attained the character of force; as a force, it could

119

alter the course of individuals, bend the nature of living, enhance the tone of life, and change character. For the fulfilment of vision, aspirations were reluctantly forsaken and a new mode of life taken up if necessary.

The vision as a force could alter conduct, mode of life, and even character; it wrought yet another change. For with the coming of vision, existence became living; that is, man entered a moral order where his individual acts and conduct assumed character and quality that they did not previously possess. Prior to this event, a man was, in a moral sense, incomplete, a half-being; by vision he gained purpose that conferred meaning upon his actions and unity to his life.

Purpose without quest is empty; a vision without fulfilment is vain. Just as Kitche Manitou received a vision and created matter, being, and life, so man in receiving a vision had to live it out.

Besides fulfilment, vision required preparation. The capacity for vision, like other faculties, was only a capacity whose growth required nourishment. And because man was a composite being, man's two substances needed preparation in order to attain a state of harmony necessary for reception of the vision. Not until these corporeal and incorporeal substances were ready and worthy did the vision come. Not until a man was ready to live out the vision did he receive it.

Preparation rendered the body worthy through physical testings, and the inner being worthy through dreaming and vigils ready for vision; both substances had to be worthy of each other. For the body there was to be strength, endurance, agility; for the inner being, patience, discipline, silence, and peace. Only when there was state of readiness did man receive his vision.

There were two dimensions to a man's life; one existence, the other a moral sense. By far, the most significant was the latter. The physical because of the difficulty of survival was considered to comprise four hills, infancy, youth, adulthood, and old age; the moral also consisted of the preparation, the quest, the vision, and the fulfilment which corresponded to the four physical phases.

Life was difficult in physical terms. Few survived infancy. Many more died in the stage of youth. Men and women, on attaining adulthood endured privations in discharging their duties; and in old age, they faced frailty, disappointment, deafness, and blindness. Through all stages, there was illness, frequently, hunger.

Though existence was hard, the vision had to be sought. There was no better way to achieve understanding of self and life. Moreover, it impressed merit upon a man and enabled him to endure the difficult life and to fulfil his purpose in life.

120

While it was almost mandatory for a man to seek a vision, the quest did not always lead to vision. It was a gift that came to those who were prepared and came only when man was ready.

For women there was no such comparable obligation to seek a vision. Any obligation that might have pre-existed was removed by the first of mothers, who gave birth to men and completed the cycle of life and time, creation, destruction and re-creation. By this act, a woman was complete in herself. A woman, by giving life, fulfilled the first portion and requisite of being; man had to give meaning to that gift of life. But a woman was free to quest for a vision.

The first important event in a person's life was that of getting a name. An elder, usually a grandparent of the infant, conferred the name at the request and invitation of the parents.

For boys names were drawn from the climatic conditions at the time of birth, from one of the aspects of the galaxy, or from animals reflecting the disposition or the anticipated character of the child. For girls, the names were derived from plants, especially flowers, the phases of solar time, and the conditions and varying qualities of water, lakes, and streams. The name was especially cherished because it was in the nature of a gift of the people, bestowed through an elder and because it was in the nature of a reputation, unlike any other, and therefore unique.

Such was the mystique and force of a name that it was considered presumptuous and unbecoming, even vain, for a person to utter his own name. It was the custom for a third person, if present, to utter the name of the person to be identified. Seldom, if ever, did either husband or wife speak the name of the other in public.

Name	Meaning
Peetwaniquot — Coming Cloud	Promise, potential
Shawaegeezhig — Sloping sky	Force, strength, excellence
Misheeminauniquot — Great Good Cloud	Cheerful, joyful
Kineu — War Eagle	Courageous, foresight
Addik — Caribou	Graceful, watchfulness
Tabobandung — He who sees far	Clear thinking, judgement
Nawadjiwon — In the middle of the stream	Willingness, resourcefulness
Abeetung — He who is	Independence, freedom
Beedaubun — Coming Dawn	Hope, certainty
Waubun-anung — Morning Star	Constancy
Waubagone — Flower	Beauty, truth
Quaequaek — Ever Turning	Industriousness

With the gift of name (even though it might change later in life) a duty to espouse the ideals embodied in his name was imposed upon the infant, and upon the parents an obligation to guide the child in the pursuit of those ideals.

During the next two or three years the child lived encased in a cradle-board. It was here that the child sharpened his faculties of sight by watching birds, moving leaves, and scudding clouds; and his faculty of hearing by listening to the utterances of birds, the rustle of leaves, and the voices of men and women.

As soon as the child began to understand, training began in earnest. In this phase and those that followed, the purpose was to foster listening and dreaming. Ultimately, the goals were to enhance the capacity to receive and to instil inner peace. It was through the form of story and song that training was conducted and fostered stage by stage.

Initially, the stories were not really stories at all. Often they were simply imaginative descriptions of the appearance and conduct of the animals, plants, and men — accounts accompanied by drums and pantomime. The immediate end was to induce sleep; the more remote and ultimate object was to foster dreams, the simplest and first form of vision.

Before story, children were frequently asked questions, "What did you see today that was beautiful? What did you hear, that was pleasing? What did you touch that was moving?" Such were the ways children were encouraged and induced to look upon beings as good.

Stories were told slowly and graphically to allow a child to enkindle his imagination. There were times, even before the story was finished, the child fell asleep amused and perhaps dreaming. In these stories, there was no element of terror.

As the child grew older, the stories took on deeper meaning. Not only did the stories go beyond the child's immediate world, but they assumed a moral character. To teach the young what was considered meritorious or what reprehensible in human conduct, the grandparents as storytellers would re-create in story form the state of things in the family or community. Deliberately, the characters in the story were made to correspond to the numbers of members in the family or reflect the character of each person appearing in the account. In these stories, men, women, and children were represented as animal beings.

While the children would not immediately recognize themselves in the characters of the plot or understand the substance of the story, they would, eventually come to know themselves and the meaning of the story after repeated renditions. Young people were allowed to draw their own inferences about the sense of the story and to acquire, through their own efforts, a sense of what was considered right or wrong.

As the youngsters grew older the stories assumed even greater depth. Themes covered hunger, courage, generosity, fidelity, creation, death, the nature and essence of being, the tone of life, the quality of existence, transformation, history, and all matters that related to life and being, matters that engage the fascination of mankind. Youngsters, with older people, listened to fables, legends, myths, tragedies, comedies, and allegories.

From the story-teller the young gained insights into life. It was through story that the people grew in understanding.

About age seven, the boys left the tutelage of women and began to learn the practical arts and to prepare their physical substances. By hunting and fishing, that is, providing food for the community, the boys became an integral part of the community.

One of the great events that deserved recognition and celebration was the first game killed by a youth. To commemorate the event, to admit the youngster into the company of hunters, and to confer upon him the recognition as provider of food, a feast was given in his honour to which the entire community was invited. Following the smoking of the Pipe of Peace, there was dedication by a medicine man or other respected elder and speeches by hunters. At the feast, all present were given a portion of the game killed that had been cooked by the boy's mother. Then there was dance.

Over the next few years the young hunter accompanied his father on hunting and fishing expeditions, learning by observation how to fashion bows and arrows, stalk game, set snares and traps, and repair his equipment. Eventually able to perform many tasks, the young man became more resourceful and self-sufficient.

Between the ages of fourteen and sixteen, many young men accompanied their fathers and other warriors on the war-path when one was undertaken. On these occasions, the young men watched in order to learn.

When boys were not engaged in hunting or fishing or any other occupations, they wrestled, ran races, swam in cold water, or went without clothing in frigid weather to develop discipline, endurance, and perseverance as part of the preparation for the quest.

The boys received one form of training; the girls another. But while the end of training for the girls was different from that of the boys, the form and the mode of training that they received nevertheless enabled those who chose to quest for the vision to attain it.

Women had a sphere in life not less essential for the well being of family and community than that of men. Within that sphere women had scope for self-fulfilment and growth. Outside of and connected with their spheres, they were to become companions just as men were expected to become companions. It is significant that the term "weedjeewaugun" — companion in life — applied equally to both men and women who became companions.

As a companion a woman was to develop cheerfulness; as a mother, industriousness. In her own right, a woman sought fortitude, self-reliance, and patience to enable her to discharge her duties to family and community and to fulfil herself.

Women were of the substance and quality of the earth, abiding. Like the earth they endured changes and challenged life as they sought peace.

When the boys at age seven or thereabouts received their first bows and arrows, the girls received a wooden doll carved either by her father or grandfather. The doll was not only a toy but a means of training as well. Through talking and telling stories to the doll, a girl acquired the art of story telling and a mastery of language, faculties that would serve her later in life as a teacher.

At the same time training was pragmatic. For the girl, the day was spent helping her mother. She kept the lodge clean by sweeping, and she folded and placed blankets and packages in their proper places. Even the immediate area around the lodge was kept tidy. The girl gathered wood, fetched water, watched her younger brothers and sisters; she watched the cooking of food, washed the utensils after meals. Besides these tasks, she gathered berries, vegetables, plants, birch bark. And when she was not occupied with some work, she watched the women making baskets or preparing hides, learned how to sew and repair garments and absorbed the stories told by the elder women.

Through all these tasks the little girl was made to feel to be an integral part of the family. In the tasks that she undertook, her grandmother or mother would say to her, "We will clean the lodge," or "We will mend father's coat," or "We will help grandmother." It was in such a manner that industry was fostered along with cheerfulness.

For a girl the attainment of womanhood was the most singular event in her life; it was the greatest of gifts.

When her time came, around her twelfth year, the girl was removed from the village and lodged in a shelter constructed for her. For a period, lasting between four and eight days the girl abstained from food, taking only water to sustain her. Her only visitor was her mother or her grandmother.

So unique and personal was the gift of life-giving considered that young girls were placed in solitude during the receipt of gift and empowerment. The gift the young girl was receiving was the personal gift of Kitche Manitou. Consequently, the girl had to prepare by vigil, the reception. Her mood and spirit were to be prepared fitting for the nature of the gift. There was to be no distraction; hence no food; there was to be no interference; hence no visitors. And because the gift was intended for women alone, there were to be no men. The gift was denied to men ever to remain a mystery, sealed and closed.

When the vigil was over the girl was no longer a child, she was a woman by transformation. She was now able to conceive and give birth; she possessed a gift which she had not possessed before. Ready and changed, the girl was returned to her home and village by her mother where a feast awaited her.

While girls attained womanhood early and assumed their place in the physical and moral orders, boys were only beginning to seek their destinies and purposes in life.

The Quest

In their twelfth year boys were deemed ready to begin their quest for vision. After purification ceremonies, a boy was conducted by his father to a place of visions, a remote, solitary place, unique by virtue of its mood and spirit for the reception. There, the boy was left alone in a specially constructed lodge, to contemplate life, his being, and existence. In solitude he endeavoured to bring his inner being and body together in accord as he attempted at the same time to be conjoined with the earth and the animal creatures and plant beings who resided in the place of vision. To be at one with the world, or to discover one's meaning through peace and silence, was not easy.

For some, the vision came early, ending the quest and inaugurating a new phase of life, being. For others, the vision came late.

Whether the boy had received his vision or not at age sixteen, he received from his mother, a three-cornered blanket which served as his coat, blanket covering, and cushion. The blanket was a gift, a symbol of love and an emblem of an attachment. With the gift of blanket was signified partial dependence, partial independence. The young man was now on his own, independent. After this he could set up his own shelter as it pleased him. As the blanket was incomplete, it symbolized a bond, a sign of continuing motherhood.

Until a young man had performed an act of courage, he was considered physically a boy. It was act of courage that admitted him into the company of warriors and gave him the status of manhood. And there was no better way of demonstrating physical quality and worth than by exposure to injury and even death. Overcoming the danger entitled a man to wear a feather or a bear claw in his necklace as a symbol of his deed.

But courage was more than a single act of bravery. It was an attribute of manhood that was almost synonymous with the term man. In some instances, courage or some proof of courage was required of a young man before marriage. With the performance of the first brave deed, a man embarked upon a course in which courage would become a part of his being.

Through this stage of preparation, those who had not attained the vision continued the quest annually in summer.

Before going out to the place of visions to keep vigil, the vision seeker first had to cleanse his body in the purification lodge. There, his body would be cleansed by vapours created from the four primal elements: fire, rock, water, and the breath of life; the soul-spirit was cleansed by contemplation and denial and privation.

Then for four days or until the vision, the questor remained in vigil abstaining from food. Man's soul-spirit hunger had to be filled; his bodily hunger more easily fed, could wait. There was to be no distraction; no weakening of resolve. Food had to be forsaken. The vision seeker had to surrender completely to self and to the place around him.

In silence, and peace would vision come to him who was prepared.

The Vision

The Anishnabeg recognized at least three kinds of vision, the distinction based upon the mode of coming of the vision. In form and nature, the different visions were similar.

By Waussayauh-bindumiwin was meant vision that was received during vigil and whose meaning was complete. No further or additional visions were required. The message was unified.

The word Waussayauh-bindumiwin issues from two terms; the first, waussayauh, meaning, light and clarity; the second, inaubindum, meaning perception by sight or insight. Within the context of the purpose, nature, and essence of vision, waussayauh-bindumiwin means many things; self-understanding, enlightenment of self, while at the same time, suggesting destiny and even career.

But not all visions came complete and entire. Perhaps the majority were of the kind known as "mauzzaubindumiwin"; that is, unclear and incomplete. A vision could come in stages under different circumstances and over a long period. Only after a number of partial visions had been received would the entire vision become clear.

The term, mauzzaubindumiwin itself means hazy or fuzzy and even vague, owing probably to the incomplete nature of the various portions of the vision received.

In form, nature, and mode, the "apowawin" is similar to the waussayauh-bindumiwin. Like the waussayauh-bindumiwin, it is complete. It differs only in that it comes during sleep. Because it occurs during sleep often rousing the dreamer to consciousness and because it makes the dreamer aware of himself, the term means "awakening" or self-revelation.

Self-revelation or awakening could come to either man or woman; it was not necessarily the privy of man. But when it did come, it was regarded as personal not to be disclosed to others; nor were others to interfere with the vision or the quest of another person. It was said "Do not give away your soul-spirit; Do not attempt to enter the soul-spirit of another." To reveal one's spirit was tantamount to surrender of self and a loss of freedom. An attempt to enter the inner being of another person was construed as an act of possession.

The individual and his individuality were inviolable; his vision was equally inviolable. No person was to surrender to another; no person was to seek dominion over another man or woman. The principle was binding.

The following stories illustrate the principles stated above and by implication, many others.

"Waubosse" — White Rabbit

Waubosse was a young maiden who chose to seek a vision. She was about fourteen when she began her quest.

On the occasion of the reception of her vision, Waubosse had kept vigil for six days. During her watch, she heard a supra-natural voice emanating from the heavens inviting her to walk the Shining Trail which led from the earth skyward to some point beyond the furthest star. As invited, Waubosse ascended the path into space walking until she met Everlasting Standing Woman who took her hand and conducted her to Little Man Spirit. The young lady was then escorted by these beings to the abiding place of Bright Blue Sky. Though she did not meet or see Bright Blue Sky, she heard him say:

You will give new voices
You will extend the green

You will give new breath
You will give new branches

The voice vanished as an echoed whisper, leaving Waubosse bewildered as to the meaning.

When Waubosse awakened from her dream, she saw a great moon enter her lodge. A voice from within the sphere chanted, "You shall see far; you shall hear far; you shall hear things afar; you shall feel things not near; you shall sense things unmoved and unformed."

Young Waubosse did not immediately understand what the dream portended. It was only after considerable thought and guidance that the young maiden realized that she had been given power to heal and to see into the future.

Pitchi-Robin

Ten years elapsed before Menominee (Rice) and his wife, Nado-waequae, (Iroquois Woman) became parents of a boy. Having been disappointed to despair by years of hoping, the couple were overjoyed. They both aspired for their son from the very first. In fact, they became so inordinately pleased, not only with their son, but also with themselves that they harboured all manners of hopes for their son. While the mother doted upon her infant son, the father nurtured ambitions.

By the time the boy was seven, Menominee had determined what his son would be and what he would do to attain his end. More than anything else, Menominee wanted his son to excel over all other young men in the village in hunting, fishing, fighting, racing, shooting, and in all physical skills. Menominee's son would be the first man.

In the years that followed, the training Menominee inposed upon his son was intense. But in one respect, Menominee failed. Although the boy developed remarkably and amazed the village, the boy did not foster a mean disposition, an essential part of the character of warriors.

And although swimming, wrestling, and shooting contests pleased the boy, he much preferred to listen to the songs of birds and to hear the chants of singers and to dance to the beat of drums. Secretly, he aspired to chant and to make people happy, through music and dance. Still he tried to please his father.

When the time for contests arrived, the boy did not, even though he excelled, triumph or win in every instance. It was true he was victorious in most matches, but he lost a few times.

To come first or to be victorious in the majority of encounters was not good enough for Menominee. He drove and urged his son to greater efforts, and try as he might, the boy could not

128

overcome his lack of strength. He was born of average size and docile disposition.

When the boy triumphed, there was joy; when he failed, desolation. On occasions of defeat, Menominee would reproach his son bitterly and refuse to speak to him sometimes for days. For the boy, the only solace was in listening to the songs of birds. There was no gratification in triumph; dread in losing.

Eventually, Menominee realized that his son would never, as he had hoped, be the foremost man in the community. But mediocrity in the physical order, Menominee reasoned, did not preclude excellence in the moral order. The father, therefore, determined that his son would excel through vision.

With a change in ambition, came change in father's attitude. He now encouraged his son to seek vision.

The boy was glad, his time was near in any event. At his father's direction, the boy went out to the Place of Vision. The first vigil was abortive, there was no vision. Nor did the second vigil produce vision. Five years came, lingered, went; nothing.

At first, Menominee said nothing about the failures; but as time passed, Menominee's solicitude turned to contempt and bitterness and he began to consider his son to be somewhat unworthy, while the boy began to despond.

Nevertheless, father and son persevered. In the spring of the sixth year of quest, Menominee said to his son as they were setting out for the Place of Vision, "I don't know why you have not yet had your vision. Most young men your age have received theirs." The lodge was set up and the father withdrew.

Four days later bringing meat and corn to feed his son, Menominee returned to the Place of Visions. As he approached, the lodge whose entrance was open, Menominee sensed that something was wrong. There was no sound, no sign of life. He looked into the lodge which was stark and empty. Anxious, Menominee looked around before calling out. But there was no reply to his shout except the echo of his voice resounding throughout the forest. All that day, he searched and shouted.

Exhausted, despondent, and sensing the worst, Menominee abandoned his search late that evening. On his tearful way home, a little bird, black of head, orange of breast, and a dark grey, followed the dejected man. Flitting from tree to tree the strange little bird accompanied Menominee home, singing all the while.

Near Menominee's lodge, the little bird made his nest and chanted daily afterward, morning and evening.

Next day and for weeks after, Menominee went back to the Place of Vision to resume his search for his son. His only and ever constant companion was the little bird who went with him every time he returned to the Place of Vision.

Eventually, Menominee despaired of ever seeing his son again. Still, over the years, the man returned to the Place of Vision almost daily, often to sit in gloom. And as often as he went, the little bird accompanied him. Eventually, too, Menominee found solace in the little bird who was his companion.

And even though time passed, Menominee's sense of loss did not diminish. He, very old and frail, continued to go frequently to the Place.

One day, tired from the walk and weary, Menominee fell asleep upon the grasses at the Place of Visions. He dreamed. And in his dream, he saw his son descend from another sphere, and stand beside him. Holding up his hand as in greeting, the boy, youthful and happy, spoke.

"Father, I'm glad that you have come. I have waited for a long time to see you here. Only here, where our paths once parted a long time ago could we meet. I am glad that we met because now I can tell you that I love you. Since that day when I received my vision, I have been sad for you. When I was a boy I loved you and tried to make you happy, but I could not. You too loved me; tried to make me happy but could not. In my quest, I asked for the ability to please you, at the same time, bring happiness to our people and peace to myself.

"During my quest, I was suddenly enveloped by a brilliant orange light as blinding as the sun. The light itself was circumscribed by dark grey and crowned by black. At the same time I was suffused by song and music which touched and moved my innermost soul-spirit. When I opened my eyes, I was soaring in the skies; tired, I rested upon a tree and sang the state of my soul-spirit which was filled with happiness. I learned then that song is the utterance of the soul-spirit. I knew then that I could move you, touch men, women, and children and by so doing, bring gladness to myself in form proper to my being and aspirations.

"On the day of my vision and transformation I saw you come; I heard you call; I followed you in your quest for me. I met you but you did not see me. I answered your call but you did not hear.

"I saw and felt your sorrow. In time your grief diminished; and you found, as I did, solace in music. I was glad. At last I could bring you some happiness. Now, father, as a bird, I shall continue to live near you and the Anishnabeg; as 'pitchi,' robin, I shall make you glad. I leave you now."

Menominee woke up. And with his awakening vanished the

anguish that had burdened him over the years. He saw himself.

What the old man learned from his bitter experience he now imparted to his fellow Anishnabeg.

Never interfere with the vision quest of another.
Never allow another to interfere in your quest.
Love your children for what they are; not for what they can do.
Do not aspire beyond your scope and your own being.

When the old man died, he was met by his son in the Land of Souls; Pitchi's son and daughters continued to sing to the Anishnabeg.

Kineu — Eagle

To some, visions came early; to others, late. But until men received their visions, they were regarded as youths, still in the second stage of life, preparing. Not to have received a vision was no reflection upon a man.

Such was the experience of Kineu, a renowned warrior who, from youth, had always demonstrated his dauntlessness. An outstanding fighter and leader, he conducted numerous war expeditions against hostile war parties. In the majority of these encounters, Kineu's warriors were victorious. His returning warriors brought back many honours entitling them to wear eagle plumes as marks of their courage and deeds. Warriors crowded to Kineu to share in the honours and to accompany him on his expeditions. For the few casualties that his warriors suffered, Kineu was respected.

In only one respect was Kineu's life and career incomplete. Although nearly fifty years old, he had not attained his vision. What he had accomplished meant nothing.

However, during the summer of his fiftieth year of life, Kineu received his vision. In it he saw the Pipe of Peace, the enemies that he had slain embracing his warriors. And he saw himself conducting the Pipe of Peace dance. As the dancing and the dancers faded, the sacred Pipe shone even brighter before fading into the sky.

Kineu was elated; yet disturbed. Did not the sacred Pipe represent peace, as did the Dance? As such, did it not portend a purpose, a theme, or even a mode of life contrary to his own mode and aspirations? How could he, Kineu, a warrior espouse a career that was opposed to what he stood for? How could he, a man of the war-club, embrace an ideal and a principle and still retain his honour, integrity, and credibility? How could he, Kineu, undertake peace for which he was not prepared either by training or inclination? It was not that he was opposed to peace.

Was not peace the end of war? The vision presaged matters far beyond Kineu's aspirations and scope.

Kineu did not understand. He, therefore, sought guidance of men and women learned in such matters. He suspected the worst and the counsel that he received only confirmed what he most feared. Kineu had to renounce the war-club and espouse the Pipe of Peace. Still he hesitated. To abandon the warpath, he thought, was tantamount to cowardice. Kineu procrastinated. Kineu had to change; and that needed time. He delayed. To do good, Kineu first had to undo the evil he had done. Former enemies would have to be mollified; in the process, friends would be lost. Kineu would have to overcome distrust, to establish his sincerity. Kineu waited.

But at last Kineu cast aside his uncertainty, forever put away his war-club and his accoutrements. Nevermore, he resolved, would he go on the war-path. And though his warriors asked him for another expedition, he refused. After awhile his own people wondered and his own warriors, all former friends began to distrust him; some even considered him cowardly. What Kineu had anticipated was coming true.

Still, he persisted. Over the objections of his people and impediments put up by his former friends, Kineu endeavoured to bring peace between his people and their enemies. In doing so, he earned the censure of friends. For peace, Kineu suffered rebuffs and animosity. Only after many years, was he accepted and trusted for what he was and for what he tried to do. No longer a man of war, he was now a man of peace.

The story of Kineu portrays the force of vision.

In the physical order, "vision" was a dramatic revelation of purpose, character and sometimes avocation. In the moral order, "vision" was a birth, a becoming. According to the Anishnabeg, from the moment of vision, a man began "to be," he was no longer a youth but an adult. At that moment, a man's acts and conduct assumed quality; purpose conferred character. Having received a vision, a man had then to live it out: considered in yet another aspect, a man had to be true to his vision.

As vision was of supernatural order and nature and personal in scope, it demanded fulfilment. And while the general content and theme of a vision might be deduced from the conduct of a person, recipients did not disclose their visions. The soul spirit was inviolate.

LIVING OUT THE VISION

Living out the vision was not less difficult than the quest. Men made errors in judgement; they forgot. That the Path of Life was tortuous was portrayed on birch bark scrolls — seven and sometimes nine branches digressed from the main road. Men and women straying from the main road were considered to have betrayed their vision; such a state was tantamount to non-living in which acts and conduct had no quality. To avoid such a state, men and women went on annual retreat to review their lives to find where they had strayed, and to resume the true path.

Man in the last phase of life, old age, was considered to have acquired some wisdom by virtue of his living on and by fidelity to his vision. Wisdom was knowing and living out the principles of life as understood.

Ceremonies, Songs, Dances

> In my song you hear my soul-spirit
> In my dance, see its rhythm
> In my ceremony, feel its depth.

Of the many ceremonies performed and observed by the Anishnabeg during a lifetime and in the course of a year none was more essential or as replete with meaning as was the Pipe of Peace smoking ceremony. It could be held alone, but no other ceremony commenced without first the Smoking of the Pipe.

Before a Council, Dance, Festival, Midewewin, First Kill, Raven, Dog Festival, Feast of the Dead, Thanksgiving, Funeral, or Marriage service could begin, the Pipe had first to be smoked. Without the smoking, the ceremony that followed would seem incomplete.

Nor had any other ceremony meanings comparable in scope and depth to that of the Pipe. Other rituals had limited meaning and application. Only the Pipe ceremony possessed a universal and more profound meaning than other rituals. Other rituals embodied meanings and symbolized material, temporal and present relationships. The pipe represented all relationships, man to Kitche Manitou, man to the cosmos, man to the plant world, man to the animal world, man to man, man to his state, and quality of life and being and existence.

As such, the Pipe was prior in substance, nature, mood, tone, to any other ceremony. It was antecedent in time and universality. Only by relation to the broader framework and practice did other ceremonies with a narrower scope attain meaning.

PIPE OF PEACE SMOKING CEREMONY

When everyone was assembled, the celebrant, a leader, or medicine man, or a revered elder would rise. The men, women, and children, forming the outer circle, ceased talking and gave their attention to the ceremony. A nod indicated the celebrant's readiness; and, at the motion, the Keeper of the Pipe of Peace advanced and offered the pipe to the celebrant.

In the Pipe of Peace smoking ceremony were represented the four orders of life and being: earth, plant, animal, and man the celebrant. The earth, whose elemental substance was rock, made up the pipe. The plant, tobacco was the sacrificial victim. The animal was symbolized by feathers and tegument appended to the pipe and the stem.

Considered in its totality, the smoking represented man's relationships to his maker, to the world, to the plants, to the animals, and to his fellow men; in another sense, it was a petition and a thanksgiving.

In each of the acts that made up the entire ceremony, the smoking was considered to be a symbolic declaration of the beliefs and understandings about life, death, and living.

The substance used — tobacco — was the sacrificial victim, incense, and offering, all at the same time. In the immolation of the leaf, was the tangible demonstration and evidence of creation and destruction, life and death, and the change of form of all substances.

Each act in the smoking reflected some belief about some aspect of life, living, and being.

By the first act, the offering of a whiff of vapour toward the sun, the Anishnabeg did posit the existence and being of a Master of Life, Kitche Manitou. Though the smoke was breathed to the sun, the offering was, in fact, tendered to Kitche Manitou, through the sun. It was in this singular mode that the Anishnabeg acknowledged that all being and all life has its origin in and ultimately comes from Kitche Manitou; and, that the sun is the physical agency through which the Master of Life confers his goodness and generosity.

In offering the whiff to the sun, the Anishnabeg were, by implication affirming the mystery and incorporeality of Kitche Manitou. At the same time and in the same way, they were acknowledging that the Great Unknown could be known through his creations.

What was created was not so much an act of power, though it was that to be sure, but an act of generosity and an act of fulfilment of a vision. And each act of generosity had to be acknowledged in some tangible way; hence, the breath of smoke.

The second whiff of incense was to the earth. According to legend and tradition, creation began with the making of water, fire, stone, and wind. It was from these substances that the physical world of sun, moon, earth, and stars were formed. After the earth, plants were made; then, the animals; last, man. To all creatures, earth was mother. The offering of incense to the earth was an act of homage not only to the earth, but also to womanhood. In the functions of the earth were seen the gifts of life and being, the fulfilment of purpose. The earth was woman; woman, earth. Both gave birth and life, both sustained being, growth, existence; both enhanced life; finally, both were primal.

But neither earth nor woman conferred life alone. A woman, by special act with man, conceived and gave birth; the earth by mystic union with the sun, through heat and rain generated beings and upheld life.

In tendering a whisper of incense to the earth, the Anishnabeg honoured not only motherhood; they honoured life giving, the wonderful miracle that is shared by woman and man and permitted by Kitche Manitou.

As men and women honour their mothers and fathers, so ought they to pay homage to the sun and earth.

And just as the first two breaths of smoke were offered in gratitude for and in acknowledgement of the origin of life and represented the attitude of men and women toward their creator and parents, so the next four whiffs blown toward the four cardinal directions that encompassed the world reflected a belief about the tone and quality of life and living and the relationships to the other orders of beings and existence.

After blowing smoke to the earth, the celebrant turned to the east and blew a puff of vapour to that point in the horizon where the sun each day rose to bring a new dawning to all beings. To the Anishnabeg, each new rising of the sun was tantamount to a new life, a time new and different from that which had passed the previous day. The day previous died with the sinking of the sun; out of the darkness rose a new time with the sun.

With the days there was a daily death and a daily birth; as there was annually dissolution and regeneration.

At dawn, the flowers opened; the birds began to sing; men and women rose refreshed, strong and ready for new life. There was in this, a miracle. For men and women and beasts the awakening from sleep, was like re-birth for the world from the state known as half-death — nebauhwin — from the bond of darkness and light. Each morning represented a new start in life, a new life to live. Men and women rising from their pallets, unburdened by weariness and sorrow went out of their lodges with hope and gratefulness in their hearts to face the east and intone a prayer of thanksgiving.

The miracle that daily and annually occurred in the physical order also took place in the human order. The birth of a child was analagous to the coming of the dawn for the joy and hope it brought. Like the new day the child has a life to live and purpose to fulfil. And like a new day that replaces the one passed, the infant in time will take the place of his parents and carry on and take up life. Such are the bonds between the present and the future. Men and women must labour for children, because in the children will the spirit of the people continue to reside and through their lives be transmitted and enhanced in succeeding generations.

The young for their part must grow in wisdom and fulfil the wonderful promise of their birth and youth; otherwise, the promise and freshness is a nullity.

Birth and infancy is but one stage in the course of life. It is no more important than are the other phases of being and existence. For a full and complete life, three other stages, youth, adulthood, and old age must be traversed. During his progression from one phase to the next a man and woman must seek wisdom and self fulfilment so that in the later stages of life, he will have something to offer to his fellow man and to his community.

Then is offered a breath of incense to the west, to that point in the encompassed world where each day the sun sinks and the world loses light. With the waning of light the flowers enfold themselves, the birds cease their singing, and men yield to sleep.

Similarly, in the human or moral order, men live out their lives, grow weak in decrepitude, and then expire. When man dies, he is said to have taken a journey to the west to disappear like the sun over the edge of the world.

At death, the body of the deceased is placed upon a platform with the feet pointed to the west, and the body exposed to enable the soul-spirit to leave its corporeal frame.

Man is a composite being, made up of a corporeal substance that is finite, and an incorporeal substance which is immortal and capable of growth. And it is the incorporeal substance that needs growth in all its aspects during its mortal existence; and, that growth ought to have as its end and purpose, inner peace or accord between heart and mind. There must be a union of all parts of the inner being and, paradoxical as it may seem, union between two contrary substances.

There is upon man and woman an obligation to develop or enhance the soul-spirit, the incorporeal substance. At the same time, the obligation to enlarge, is a challenge. The soul-spirit

137

appears to be one and indivisible, however, it operates under different modes and aspects. To enlarge and foster the inner being imposes upon a person a duty to know and understand his inner being. And because every man and woman is endowed with different powers and gifts of insight and understanding, only the individual, and no other, is deemed capable of understanding himself and directing the growth of his inner self. On this basis, no person interfered in the self-growth of another. A man or woman alone was accountable for his self-development.

When a person has lived out his term of life upon earth and has been measured by the good performed or by the duration of existence from youth to old age, he then may enter Land of Souls in peace.

Were a person to die before the term of life allotted to him expired, or, if he died without having done sufficient good, or, if he died in a state of inner turmoil, he would not find acceptance in the Land of Souls among the soul-spirits beings at peace. According to some accounts, the soul-spirit meeting rejection returns to earth seeking to infuse another being in the physical world or exist in exile outside the community of the Land of Souls and the Land of the Living.

From the west, the first celebrant turned, and offered a breath to the north, the abode of winter and the source of the perilous way. For the people of the north who annually had to face and endure privation and the ravages of winter, life was an ordeal; for men and women questing for and seeking to live out their visions, life was painful. Even the spirits and the gods, though empowered by supernatural abilities, encountered sufferings in the physical and moral senses.

To face the hardships of the ever-changing climate, the extremes of winter, and often the scarcity of food, men and women had to develop courage, fortitude, endurance, patience, perseverance, cheerfulness, generosity, resourcefulness. But more than that, there was need to understand the laws that governed nature and the other beings, and obligation to regulate life in accordance with the changes of the seasons and according to the understanding of the laws of the world.

It was not easy to undersand the laws. Nevertheless, in considering the laws that governed the physical world, the Anishnabeg posited primal laws that regulated the movement of cosmic bodies, the coming and going of the seasons, the wax and wane of light and darkness, the division of rock, fire, water, and wind. All other laws were predicated upon and were subsidiary to the first laws.

The events of the world and sequence of life and being

followed an order that was based upon the primary world laws. Each species had his sphere. Life proceeded from birth, through growth to decay, and ended in death. Such was the natural sequence and order prescribed by the first laws. There was harmony between the operations of the secondary laws and the primary.

Men were dependent for their well-being upon the harmonious operations of laws, primary and secondary; and upon the cosmic bodies and species remaining within their proper spheres. And though the seasons, days and nights tended toward balance, there were times when the winters were too long and the days too cold. There were occasions when too much rain fell and killed everything; when the sun shone too hot destroying too much; when excessive variations took place, birth, growth, fullness were in the plant and animal orders delayed, obstructed, and even impaired. Over such changes, man had no control; he had to endure and labour and adjust to the changes.

Life was an ordeal. For leaders, the whiff of smoke to the north served as a reminder that decisions made in their councils were to be based on the principle "that the well-being of people took precedence over form, custom, and even tradition." Leaders were to avoid making conditions and matters worse for families and community; and, during the smoking, leaders petitioned Kitche Manitou for wisdom. With wisdom and prudence, decisions made would render life just a little more bearable.

Life was an ordeal, not only in the physical sense, but in a moral sense as well. Central to the life of the Anishnabeg was the "vision." The first portion of life, infancy and youth, was a period of preparation and quest for the vision. Both were arduous. Both body and soul-spirit had to be prepared and tested. Only when both were made fit by frequent testing did the vision come. After vision, in the adult and old age stages of life, came the period of understanding and living out the vision. Neither was easy. Perhaps the ordeal in the moral order was more demanding than that in the physical order.

Ordeal though the preparation and quest might have been, it was the vision that wrought profound changes in the tone, quality, and style of a man's life. For prior to the vision, life was existence, preparation and receiving; after vision, life became living, fidelity, and giving.

The final whiff of tobacco incense was drawn and offered to the south. This was the act that embodied thanksgiving for all temporal gifts and good. To the Anishnabeg, the south was the image of summer, birth, growth, and fulfilment; its colours were green and yellow. With the coming of spring and summer ended the hardship of winter. Men and women offered thanksgiving for the survival and heralded the advent of summer; at the end of summer, they again celebrated a thanksgiving for the bounty of the summer. For gifts, there was need for thanks. Men looked to the south for growth of food, the song of bird, the return of game, the end of winter's constraints, and a new beginning in freedom.

Men rejoice in witnessing in the cycle of time in the physical world the mystery of birth, re-birth, the miracle of new life, growth and self-healing. For it is only by seeing in the physical order, birth and death, beginning and end, that life can be understood and appreciated. For a man whose life and time is linear, there is no re-birth in the physical order. There is an end to physical existence at death; then a passage to and perhaps admission into the Land of Souls, a new and different existence, where even the essence and nature of man's soul-spirit changes. The physical ordeal ends with winter and the better life comes with summer.

Thus in part is the meaning of the Pipe of Peace Smoking Ceremony. It could be held on its own as a ceremony, but it usually formed part of or preceded another ceremony to give meaning.

DANCE OF THE PIPE OF PEACE

Each spring the sacred pipe was removed from its casement to be renewed and regenerated. Only the keeper of the pipe (oshkawbaewis) could perform this ceremony. And as he opened the bundle to expose the pipe to the sun and to the eyes of men, he chanted prayers re-dedicating, re-sanctifying, and consecrating the pipe to the mood and spirit of peace.

The presiding medicine man then invoked the peace of Kitche Manitou and of the world to enter and infuse the pipe.

There was prayer and there was chant. Then the medicine man took up the pipe again, offered it skyward, earthward, and to the four points of the world, and began his dance around the central fire. After he had completed his circuit around the fire, the medicine man held the pipe in both his hands, and passed the sacred pipe to the next person. And so the pipe went from person to person until all had touched and been touched by the pipe.

From the sun's rays the pipe received a portion of the power of the sun and the earth; from men and women, a human peace. The pipe was by touch and intent consecrated by all. It possessed the spirit and medicine of peace. In turn, the pipe imparted peace to all who touched it.

140

Its power of peace restored and re-affirmed by ritual, real and symbolic, the pipe was restored to its casement by its keeper.

There was yet another form of dance in which the pipe was consecrated to peace and its power of peace renewed for another year. The celebrants sat in a circle around the fire. A prayer of dedication was intoned during which time the sacred pipe was held in the hands of the principal medicine man. Then, while chanting, the medicine man elevated the pipe causing it to move in dance form in front of him. The dance motion of the pipe represented the motion of the world and the pace of time. The Dance of the Pipe continued until all present had danced the pipe.

LIFE COMMEMORATIONS

During a lifetime a person would celebrate either as a principal or as a participant in a number of ceremonies marking an event or milestone.

The Naming Ceremony

The naming ceremony itself was simple. It consisted of the presentation of the child by the parents to the elder who was to give the name. The name-giver said, "You shall be called . . .", wished the child long life, and reminded the child of his duties toward his parents and totemic group.

" '—' shall be your name. It is yours. It is our gift to you. By this name, we shall know you. You must uphold this name; you must espouse ideals in this name." The name giver then presented the child to the elders.

As the child is handed to him, each elder embraces the infant and presses his cheeks against the child's face. Acceptance of the child by the elders is thus symbolically shown; there is at the same time, an unspoken commitment on the part of the elders to teach the child and impart to him their wisdom. Each person offers a blessing and his love in a prayer that he intones; each person petitions Kitche Manitou for long life for the infant.

The name conferred was more than just a term uttered to identify someone. It was also a reputation and a term which embodied his character. It was personal and, therefore to be upheld.

A name under these circumstances could be temporary or permanent. Circumstances and events occurring in later life that altered the image, character, or reputation of a person may produce a change in name. Sometimes a new name superseded the old. Such was the force of name and reputation.

The First Kill — Oshki-Nitawgaewin

As soon as a boy had killed his first game bird or animal, he presented it to his mother. Invitations were immediately sent to the entire community to celebrate the occasion and to attend the feast later that day.

At the feast, all the people received a small portion of the meat, not so much to allay their hunger but as a symbol of acceptance of the offering of the newest hunter among them. At the same time the feast that was given marked an event separating one stage in the life in human individual development, an induction and confirmation of the boy as a fully accredited hunter upon whom the family and village could rely.

Following the meal, the Pipe of Peace was smoked. Afterwards story tellers told tales of hunting and animals for the benefit of the new member of the hunters. The hunters pledged to assist the boy.

The celebration concluded with dances representing a hunt or enacting the habits and conduct of game animals.

Womanhood

When the vigil for womanhood was over the girl was returned to her home and village by her mother where a feast awaited her.

At the feast an elder welcomed her saying "you left as a girl; you return as a woman. We sorrowed when you departed, leaving behind a girlhood we had grown to love. We rejoice at your return, new and different. Through you, will the people live and live on."

The elder lady then embraced the young woman; in like fashion the other women welcomed the young woman into womanhood.

Blanket Presentation

In his sixteenth year, a young man received a three-cornered blanket from his mother to serve as his coat, pillow, and blanket. The presentation of blanket was not conducted with much formality or ceremony. It was a matter between mother and son.

Marriage

To seek and take a companion in life, either wife or husband (weedjeewaugun) was a grave undertaking.

A partner in life might be selected by the parents for their children or the young might choose their own life companions. Even if the young were to seek marriage through love, approval and permission of the parents were still needed. Marriage was permitted when totemic relationship did not form an impedment; and, in many instances, only after the young man had proved by living in the home of the girl's parents and supporting the family that he was capable of providing adequately for a future wife. But a marriage prearranged by parents was preferred.

There were other minor customs. In some cases and areas, a young man had to perform an act of courage before he could presume to court a young woman; that is, he had to be a warrior. Without some badge of bravery, a young man was deemed by girls to be only a boy fit only for the company of his mother. When the courting became serious, the parents of the young man and woman consulted beads of corn or beans to determine the totemic relationships of the young.

The marriage ceremony itself was simple in form, consisting of the sewing of either the hems or sleeves of the garments of the young. The attachment of the garments symbolized the union of two people as man and wife and represented the permanence of such bond. For the Anishnabeg marriage was a promise to be fulfilled; and though either party could terminate the marriage by placing the personal belongings of the other outside the lodge prior to the birth of children, separation or divorce was rare afer the arrival of infants.

Following a wedding feast, the newly married couple sometimes remained in the home of the bride's parents, but most frequently set up their own lodge.

Feast of the Dead

When death occurred, the corpse of the deceased, whether child or adult, was placed upon a platform, feet pointed to the west. The corpse remained exposed for four days to allow the soul-spirit to take leave of its physical frame. The separation was deemed reluctant and unwilling by reason of the long and natural union and the strength of the bond between a corporeal and an incorporeal substance. The soul-spirit needed time to make the final break.

For the interment the body was wrapped in birch bark, the feet pointed westward. Warriors were interred in a sitting position; all others were buried in a reclining position. And with the corpse were buried the personal effects of the deceased — his medicine bag and weapons. Over his grave the sign of his totem was inscribed upside down upon the death post. Beside the death post was a small fire that kept burning for four days to light the way of the soul-spirit during its passage along the path of souls and to keep warm remembrance.

Each autumn, the Feast of the Dead was observed in commemoration of all those who had died during the year. In all the households of the survivors a banquet was served. Invitations were extended to all the village. At the table was an extra setting for the deceased of the family. It was in this manner that the family and village demonstrated that they had not forgotten; such was the way the family showed that the spirit of the deceased still remained in the family. Families coming to the meal in the evening and partaking of the food did so in memory of the deceased and in honour of the family.

After death there was a period of mourning which in some instances extended for a period of one year. During this time, the mourner wore sombre attire and did not embellish his appearance. On the anniversary of the death of the deceased, the survivor was released from mourning by a feast. After the feast, the mourner could resume a normal life; songs and dances were performed; new clothing was put on and the person adorned for beauty.

Thanksgiving

Twice annually, in some rare cases four times, the Anishnabeg celebrated thanksgiving in ceremony. This did not replace the private acts of thanksgiving.

In the spring with the first flowing of sap, there was thanksgiving. Such a public gathering coincided with the return of the Anishnabeg to community living after a winter of isolated living in family form. The principal theme for the thanks was gratitude for survival from the ordeal of winter.

There was the smoking of the pipe; then offerings were given to Kitche Mantou. After, there was a dance and chants, both embodying the theme of survival.

SPRING THANKSGIVING

We have endured
The ordeal of winter
The hunger
The winds
The pain of sickness
And lived on.

We grieve for those
Grandparents
Parents
Children and
Lovers
Who have gone.

Once again we shall
See the snows melt
Taste the flowing sap
Touch the budding seeds.
Smell the whitening flowers
Know the renewal of life.

In autumn just before the Anishnabeg went to their isolated
wintering quarters there was a thanksgiving in spirit and form
like that of the spring. Only the theme was different.

AUTUMN THANKSGIVING

The roses
Enflamed the meadows
With whites and scarlets.

The robins
Filled the summer days
With their songs.

The whitefish
Flashed their silvered tails
In lakes and streams.

The corn
Waxed firm and tall
In sun and rain

The deer
Grew sleek and fat
Upon the grasses.

Our stores are full
Our medicines are strong
Our weapons are worn
Our spirits are glad
Kitche Manitou has been kind.

Festival of the Dog

There were two forms of Dog Festivals. One was for warriors;
the other was for the people in general. In the first, the purpose
was to test, and by frequent testing to uphold the courage of
warriors. In the second, the people were reminded of famine
and survival through dance. They re-lived adversity and re-
enacted their endurance. At the same time, the dance pre-figured
future famines and petitioned for courage and endurance.

DANCES

It is said that "song is the utterance of the soul." If such is the case, then dance is the enactment of the beat of the mood of the soul. A song reflects innumerable moods; a dance may represent countless beats and various rhythms.

The life rhythm of the Anishnabeg was determined by and coincided with the cycle of the year. In the spring, when there was re-birth and renewal in the physical world, there was a renaissance and regeneration for the Anishnabeg. For both, it was a time of birth, youth, and becoming. The predominating colour of spring was green. And the hue of green came to represent new life, growth, and youth.

In a very real way, life for the Anishnabeg commenced in spring. In winter most of life's tasks were suspended or curtailed. When spring arrived with the flow of maple sap, life once more was taken up with gusto. Beginning with the spring thanksgiving, the great public dances were once again celebrated. In the spring thanksgiving, survival was acknowledged and new life was celebrated. Life was once more to be taken up in fact as in ceremony.

War Dance

The war-path like other occupations was a summer enterprise. War was suspended for the winter, and like other pursuits was resumed in the spring if it had to be taken up.

On the night before a war party set out, there was held a war dance re-enacting deeds of courage and pre-figuring victory.

A war post of living green tree was cut and then erected. A great fire was kindled. The stage was set. The sounding of the drum summoned the village to the dance. And early the war drums beat the rhythm and measure of war and the death chant.

When all the village was assembled, the war chief explained the cause of war endeavouring to persuade his listeners of the justness of the cause and trying to win support. The elders usually counselled against war. If after debate, the decision was still for war, the dance began.

For the most part, the warriors, faces painted in black and red, the colours of death and war, were young. By custom and tradition, the first to get up to commence the dance was the war chief. Brandishing a war-club, he danced around the great fire, all the while recounting his exploits for the inspiration of his followers. At the finish, he struck the war post a blow signifying the might of his prowess and the fate of the enemy. Others followed in the order of numbers of battle honours won,

146

until all the warriors had told of their exploits and struck the post, the symbolic blow of death.

At the start the drums beat softly and slowly; as the evening deepened, the drums throbbed harder and with greater intensity. When it seemed as if the dancers would be unable to keep pace with the pitch and rhythm of the pounding drums, the war chief left the circle to offer his hand to the eldest of women present. In conducting her to the dance, the leader sought endurance through the joining of the hands of young and old from her long life. It was, moreover, the hand of man espousing that of woman, the giver of life. Other women are then led to the dance; old men followed, and finally the very young joined the dance as the drums pulsated.

While the men and the warriors leaped and bounded in dance, the women glided in rhythm to the drum beats, their feet not leaving the soil. This was, to the Anishnabeg, the way of women; it was as intended by Kitche Manitou. While men make war; women seek peace; while men defy death, women challenge life; while men wish to alter life, women live with its changes. The life rhythm of women is slower and different from that of men.

Men must fulfil. It is they, and not women, who must seek fulfilment through battle.

The Victory Dance

When warriors returned from battle victorious, the triumph was commemorated by dance in which everyone took part. The dance was sometimes called, the "Call of Triumph Dance." In this dance, trophies and offerings were placed upon a post, painted in red and black. It was around this post that the dance took place.

The Deer Dance

A warrior once dreamed of a deer who danced in the heavens. In commemoration of the dream the man initiated the Deer Dance as a custom among his people. In the dance the dancers attempted to enact the character of a deer; grace, watchfulness, and gentility.

Other Dances

There were many other dances. For each there was a different theme, rhythm, and beat. The Snow-Shoe Dance represented the ordeal of the hunter in winter; the Begging Dance, the situation of the hungry; the Partridge Dance, fertility and love. In fact, there was a dance for every occasion, for every theme in man's life, each one inspired by dream or imagination.

SONGS

Songs were the utterances of the soul. As such, they evoked every theme that moved men's hearts and souls. Songs were poems chanted; they could be praises sung; they could be prayers uplifted to the spirit. Most were of a personal nature composed by an individual on the occasion of a dream, a moving event, a powerful feeling.

These songs were chanted to the beat of drum or roll of rattle at feasts, death, festivals, and other occasions.

The Incorporeal World

KITCHE MANITOU

From the beginning the Anishnabeg posited the existence of Kitche Manitou, the Maker of Makers, the Master of Life, the mystery of mysteries. Unseen, Kitche Manitou could be known only through his creations, the order of the world, and the order of causes.

In the physical world the sun was the symbol of Kitche Manitou. In the Midewewin and birch-bark scrolls, Kitche Manitou was depicted as a circle with four projections.

The circle was in one sense, a path without a beginning or even a path without an end, implying eternity, enclosure, completeness, perfect unity.

The four projections symbolized the universal presence of Kitche Manitou, in all places and at all times.

He was the Master of Life who gave life and being; he gave and permitted all things. He was daily, therefore, to be thanked for life, light, and gifts.

FATHER SUN

The sun represented Kitche Manitou and the powers of giving light for guidance and heat for growth.

NOKOMIS – GRANDMOTHER TO ALL

Man's first mother was a supernatural being who resided alone in the heavens. Lonely, she asked for a companion. Kitche Manitou, feeling pity for the sky-woman sent her a consort by whom she conceived. But as soon as sky-woman conceived, her companion left her. Eventually, she gave birth to twins, who destroyed one another, leaving her alone once more.

Sky-woman, having lost love, companionship, and the gift of life through birth, desponded. Kitche Manitou again sent a companion to sky-woman. From the union that took place were born the Anishnabeg on earth.

Sky-woman remained on earth until the first Anishnabeg were able to care for themselves. Then she ascended into the heavens to return to her abode. Her existence, her gift of life, and the primacy of women are remembered each time the moon shines.

THE THUNDERS

Fewer and less familiar than grandmothers are grandfathers represented by the thunders. Grandmothers are closer and more familiar to children than grandfathers. By custom, grandmothers assisted their daughters in the care of children. They were constant companions and were ever present in the homes.

The grandfathers, on the other hand, in life and in death, were more likely to be forgotten. They too deserved remembrance and some form of homage for their love. That they be remembered, the thunders and concomitant lightnings were chosen to represent them.

Thunders came to represent powers and forces of a supernatural nature and character. These were powers over which man had no control but which governed the quality of his existence and that of the animal and plant orders. The thunders were the patrons of medicine men and women whose powers to heal were singular, striking, and conferred only upon a few.

EPINGISHMOOK

Epingishmook was the spirit husband of Winonah and father of Mudjeekawis, Papeekawis, Chibiabos, and Nanabush.

Epingishmook married Winonah and remained with her until the birth of Nanabush. After Nanabush was born, it was said that Epingishmook abandoned his wife. Not long after that Winonah died. Some said that she died of grief; others said that Epingishmook caused her death. In any event, Epingishmook left his wife and child, the land of the Anishnabeg, retiring to the land of the Mountains.

When Winonah died, Nanabush, still young, was raised by his grandmother.

Epingishmook was a spirit. As such he was an immortal being. At the same time, he had a physical aspect about him which rendered him vulnerable to flint. Though he could be injured he could not be killed.

When Nanabush learned that Epingishmook might have caused his mother's death, he sought out his father for revenge.

In his battle with his son Nanabush, it was Epingishmook's one physical weakness that led to his injury. Even though Epingishmook was wounded in the battle, he did not consider the fight as a loss; rather as an injury to bring the fight to an end.

Hateful Epingishmook might have been for leaving his wife and child, Nanabush respected him for the wisdom that he had about life. In telling his son that, "you will never gain love by killing me," Epingishmook was saying that "vengeance never brings satisfaction."

It was from Epingishmook that Nanabush received the gift of tobacco, the Pipe of Peace and the ceremony of the Pipe of Peace Smoking. Nanabush received from his father the counsel to live out his destiny, to fulfil his work and not to be diverted by sense of personal affront or gain.

WINONAH

Mother of Nanabush, a human being. Her name means "to nourish from a breast." Though she was the mother of four incorporeal beings, she was not taken as a spirit herself.

According to legend, Winonah was walking in a meadow by herself. Winonah had been warned by her mother not to go wandering by herself in the field, but to remain close to home. She was to have married a man of her parents choosing so that through marriage love would be attained. But instead, Winonah, upon meeting Epingishmook, fell in love with a spirit and married him. As either reward or punishment for falling in love with the spirit, she was unable to retain either his love or his companionship. In the end, she lost his love and his company and died of grief.

MUDJEEKAWIS

Mudjeekawis was the first born son of Epingishmook and Winonah. The name implies and means "eldest son."

He was the favourite son of Epingishmook because he went to live with his father and shared the realm of the Land of Mountains. By the time Nanabush was born, Mudjeekawis was grown up and gone. Only later did Nanabush learn about his father and brothers from his grandmother.

During his sojourn in the Land of the Anishnabeg, Mudjeekawis did much travelling, but he left behind certain legacies to the Anishnabeg.

Mudjeekawis, as a young lad, accompanied his father in all

his expeditions and acquired from him, a *wanderlust*. As soon as he was old enough, Mudjeekawis left home to roam the world in search of adventures. Only on occasion did he come back to visit his mother.

Mudjeekawis roamed the world. He went south and east. He was familiar with the eternal summer and the never-fading greens of the tropics and with the everlasting snows and barrens of the north. His favourite country was that around the Great Lakes where the climates were variable; where the country was elegant; where the game was abundant. He often told his grandmother that no country was as fair or as bountiful as the country of the Anishnabeg.

What Mudjeekawis did was to bring back stories about other lands and other peoples to the Anishnabeg. Sometimes he brought back other customs and traditions to become part of the life of the Anishnabeg.

It was Mudjeekawis who brought the wampum to the Anishnabeg.

On one of his numerous expeditions out west to the Land of Mountains and even further north, Mudjeekawis came upon a large village of great brown bears, bigger than any that he had ever seen before. When he came upon the bears, they were holding a conference. And, as each bear rose to speak, he held a belt-like sash in his hand. During the speech, the speaker often looked at the sash and pointed to it. And each was different. Some of the sashes were quite short; some quite long; some were made of bead-like shells with designs upon them; others were made of quills coloured and engraved with figures and images.

Mudjeekawis was intrigued. After the meeting he approached one of the bears for an explanation of the meaning and purpose of the sash. Told that it was a means by which the past was remembered and passed on, and that it was called wampum, Mudjeekawis seized the sash from the grasp of the great bear and made off for the woods. The bear, enraged, called for help, as he pursued Mudjeekawis, up and down the mountains heading always toward the east.

Though Mudjeekawis was small and quick and fast, he could not escape the great bear who was gaining upon him. Eventually, caught by the bear, Mudjeekawis had to fight.

The struggle was long, bloody, and fierce; but, Mudjeekawis slew the bear in front of the other grizzlies. Then Mudjeekawis took the wampum from the vanquished grizzly.

As Mudjeekawis was about to leave, the other bears trembling, petitioned Mudjeekawis to return to be their chief. Mudjeekawis agreed.

Mudjeekawis stayed with the Anishnabeg only long enough to explain the use and the meaning of the wampum. Then he bade good-bye to his brothers, Papeekawis and Chibiabos to return to the west as Kabeyung (west wind) and as leader of the grizzly bears and to share the land of his father, Epingish-mook.

PAPEEKAWIS

Papeekawis sometimes called Yenaudizih, was a man of many accomplishments; the second of four sons of Epingishmook and Winonah.

Papeekawis loved the Anishnabeg; they, in turn, loved him.

Everyone loved Papeekawis, but for different reasons. The women loved him for his agility and elegance and fineness of features.

In their admiration and love, the women made him the finest clothing, breachcloths, leggings, coats, headdresses, vests, gloves, and moccasins, embroidered and designed with flowers and symbols and worked with shells and quills. To make Papee-kawis even more handsome and striking, the women used blues, reds, and yellows in their pigments. Fond of amusement he invented many games. Besides games, he invented and designed dances and gave dances to the Anishnabeg and fostered in them, a love of dances. In fact, all the dances danced by the Anishnabeg may be attributed to the inventiveness of Papeekawis.

The men were also fond of Papeekawis although they were somewhat envious of his accomplishments. It was from Papee-kawis that they learned fine dress but also the art of certain games and amusements. As Papeekawis loved to gamble, so did the Anishnabeg. They learned the Pagaesaun (Plum Stone Game) from him and the Kindawsso, another gambling game.

Papeekawis was a great dancer, probably the greatest dancer ever known among the Ojibway. Such was the violence of his dances that he created whirlwinds, breezes, gusts, gales (warm and cold), typhoons, hurricanes. He was the patron of winds and dances, dancing for amusement and entertainment, always dancing out some drama in life.

Whenever there was celebration, Papeekawis was called to make people happy. And when his young brother, Nanabush, got married, Papeekawis was one of the principal entertainers.

And though he made people smile and laugh with his dancing, Papeekawis was a lonely man. And though he was loved by all women, no one loved him enough to marry him. He had to live alone on the southern shores of Lake Superior around Shagawawamikong. Papeekawis had a home, but he was seldom there. The lodge was cold and empty.

Papeekawis always sought and found amusement. When he didn't find it, he created amusement and often mischief and grief.

Papeekawis was fond of his brother Nanabush. Even after Nanabush got married, Papeekawis used to visit him often. One time, when he went to call on Nanabush, Nanabush and his wife were away. Papeekawis became annoyed, and in a sportive spirit caught Nanabush's beautiful white birds and painted them all black. Papeekawis waited, concealed in a bush.

Nanabush returned home with his wife and wanted to feed his white birds. When he could not find them, he became furious. Hearing Papeekawis chortle, Nanabush grew enraged. He accused Papeekawis of doing away with the birds. Papeekawis denied the accusation. Nanabush drove Papeekawis from his lodge intending vengeance.

Papeekawis fled from the lodge with Nanabush immediately behind. To escape Nanabush, who was gaining on him, Papeekawis dove into a small bush lake where he sought refuge among the beavers. He quickly explained to the beavers that an evil spirit was pursuing him and would kill him if he weren't able to escape. Papeekawis implored the beavers to help. The beavers took pity on Papeekawis and concealed him in one of their lodges.

Nanabush arrived. Knowing that Papeekawis was hidden in one of the beaver lodges, he proceeded to destroy the homes. The beaver people were convinced that Nanabush was an evil being. Consequently, when Papeekawis, terrified by Nanabush's fury, asked that he be transformed into a beaver to confuse Nanabush, the beaver people agreed and changed Papeekawis into a brother.

Even as a beaver, Papeekawis was not satisfied. His vanity exceeded his sense of well being and he requested the beaver people to make him finer and larger in stature than any other existing beaver. Again the beaver people willingly complied with the request. Papeekawis, finding himself three times larger and twice more comely than other beaver was immensely pleased and grateful.

While Papeekawis was admiring his size and beauty, Nanabush began dismembering the lodge in which Papeekawis was concealed. The other alarmed beavers escaped through the tunnels. When Papeekawis realized what was happening, he too, attempted to flee but his size prevented him from escaping. He was stuck fast at the entrance to the tunnel. It was in this awkward and embarrassing position that Papeekawis lay exposed to Nanabush.

Nanabush, finding such an enormous beaver stuck in a hole with only his broad rump protruding, knew that only his brother could be so vain and careless. Breaking down a poplar that grew on the bank of the lake, Nanabush began to thump and thwack Papeekawis' great behind intendng to scare him. But Nanabush struck him with such a force that Papeekawis shot through the tunnel into the water to the far end of the lake where he found himself among some Brant ducks.

Breathlessly Papeekawis beseeched the brants. "Help me, hide me, make me like you," rasped Papeekawis, "or else Nanabush will kill me."

The brants felt sorry and quickly changed Papeekawis into a brant. But Papeekawis was not satisfied. He was neither bigger nor more handsome than any other brant. He was too common for his vanity. He, therefore, complained to the brants "I'm too small; too plain. I should be bigger, finer in feature than any other brant."

The brants readily granted the request since nothing was lost. Immediately, Papeekawis became thrice as large as formerly and more brilliant of colour and finer of feature. He was proudly pleased with his elegance and gazed at his reflection in the water and he forgot about Nanabush.

Meanwhile Nanabush was growing angrier, having lost his quarry. In destroying the beaver lodges, he grew tired. Looking up from his labour, he spotted his brother swimming as a brant among the brants.

In a rage, Nanabush released a flight of arrows in the direction of the brants.

"Fly! Hasten! Hurry! Don't stay! Nanabush will kill us," cried out the brants as they took to the air amidst a thunderous flapping of wings. Papeekawis too, lifted off, but not without difficulty. Still he amazed himself at the ease and speed of his flight.

However, Papeekawis soon tired, began to falter. Feebly, he called out to the brants, "I'm tired." But they only urged him on. "Keep going! Don't stop! We will soon be there!" Papeekawis looked down, then shrieked, "I'm dizzy." In answer the other brants advised, "Don't look down." But Papeekawis couldn't resist. He looked down again. He got dizzy; he got sick; he plummeted to the earth.

Papeekawis's body disintegrated upon the rocks below, but his soul and spirit and shadow lived on. And being alive and needing a body, the soul and spirit and shadow of Papeekawis entered the body of a snake who was sunning himself on the rocks. The snake was startled by the invasion of soul, spirit, and shadow of another being, attempted to repel and reject the intruder. The internal struggle was so great that the snake's body coiled and writhed and twisted and knotted as in pain.

Seeing the agonized snake, Nanabush roared out, "I have found you. You cannot escape this time." And he took up a huge boulder with which to crush the snake, but the snake bolted into a great fissure, as if swallowed up by the mountain itself. Nanabush thwarted, was even more furious.

Loudly, he convoked the thunders. "Strike the rock. Demolish it to sand. The rock has been unkind."

At the request the thunders hammered the skies behind the clouds and hurled their fire arrows at the rock smashing it into sand and clouds of dust. When the dust settled down, Nanabush searched in the debris for his older brother.

Nanabush did not find his brother. All that was left was the broken, tattered, bleeding body of the snake. Nanabush realized that he had killed his brother. He wept, "No more as man, no more as animal, no more as bird, no more as snake, will you be. I did not mean to kill you. I wanted only to frighten you."

CHIBIABOS

By the time Nanabush was born, Chibiabos had grown up and gone from home. But Chibiabos did not stay away from his grandmother's lodge as his older brothers had done. He came back from time to time. Consequently, he knew his younger brother; they became constant and cheerful companions as Nanabush got older.

Chibiabos could never stay at home for long. A musician he was, cheerful and always full of laughter, and he was invited to all sorts of celebrations, festivals, and ceremonies to sing or to make music with drum, rattle, or flute. If he were not singing for people, he was singing for the grasses in the meadows, or the trees in the forest; he sang among the crags of high places, made merry music with the waters in streams and lake. He not only sang, he taught people music.

It was he who taught hunters how to imitate the calls and utterances of the animal beings. It was Chibiabos who fashioned the drums and rattles and flutes and made music, the utterances of the soul. For him, there was a song and chant for every mood, every man, every occasion.

Only one occasion is recorded on which all four brothers met. That was the day that Nanabush married. The brothers came to honour their young brother and each brother did something to amuse the crowd that gathered to celebrate. For his part, Chibiabos sang and composed songs for the happy event.

But after the wedding and reception, Mudjeekawis admonished Chibiabos for not having accomplished much and for having squandered his life. Displaying his headdress, wielding his war club, he said, "Had you been a man of courage, you would have accumulated numerous badges of courage. Instead, you have wasted your time in frivolous song. Life doesn't consist of merriment."

Chibiabos, stung, retorted, "Were you to have your way, life would be without laughter, miserable. Often I must console with song, those who have been injured by the war that you love."

"Courage makes a man; and you have not yet shown courage; you are not yet a man," Mudjeekawis taunted his young brother. And he continued, "While I have challenged and defeated all enemy warriors to make things safe for you; you have done nothing except sing and make music."

Chibiabos trembled with rage and shouted at his brother, "Name any warrior, any danger and I will show you my strength and courage."

"No one has defeated arrogant Bebon (winter)," offered Mudjeekawis. He is growing more audacious. He is chief of the Hudson and comes down as far as Temagami and Abitibi and Nipigon. I can handle him; but I would like to see what you, my brother, can do. Anyway, if you cannot defeat Bebon, I shall do it."

This last remark cut Chibiabos more than any other. Chibiabos put down his drum that he had been playing and seized a bow and arrow and a war-club. The dancing and the music ceased. And all the guests at Nanabush's wedding went down to the shore to watch Chibiabos leave to find Bebon.

The older people pleaded with Chibiabos, "Wait, don't leave now, it is too stormy." Even Mudjeekawis was alarmed, "Wait for a few days; wait until the storm is over." But Chibiabos ignored the warnings. He got in his canoe to cross the great Ojibway Lake.

Chibiabos didn't get far before his canoe was swamped by a monstrous wave and he drowned. With his death, there came a great sadness over the land.

More than any other, Nanabush felt the loss. Believing that Chibiabos could be restored to life, Nanabush convened Medicine Men and Women to recall his brother back from the bottom of the lake.

Nanabush and his colleagues chanted and sang and drummed. Immediately, the soul and spirit of Chibiabos emerged from the waves; Chibiabos had returned from death; song and music had conquered death. In remembrance of Chibiabos' return to life, he was declared to be the first of the underworld (water and earth). He was to have a place of honour in the world of the living, but he was not to enter the homes of the living. No longer did Chibiabos make music himself, but he continued to make music through rivers, leaves, trees, mountains, birds, and men. Through music, he uttered the sound of the soul.

DAEBAUDJIMOD – THE RACONTEUR

Ever since Nanabush could remember, Daebaudjimod was a frequent winter evening visitor at his grandmother's lodge. Not only was he a very special friend of the old lady; he was a masterful story-teller.

So skilled was that he could hold an audience in his hand for an evening and even for a winter. Daebaudjimod knew hundreds of stories, but even more marvellous, he could make up stories. He told real stories, he told stories that could not possibly be true. Still, people listened. He could, with stories, make people laugh and cry; he could make them wonder and think; he could make them proud by remembrance and fearful by his tales of the future.

Daebaudjimod knew all the animals, the nature of things, and all the wisdom there was to be passed on. In fact, he knew so much that no one believed him. Some called him a boaster; others challenged him to verify his stories. He often regretted that few people put much faith in his stories. Lamenting his lack of credibility he advised the young, "Do not speak too often as I have. Do not have an opinion upon every subject or matter. Do not be too facile with words and speech. Do not be too ready and willing to talk and you will be believed. Your credibility is important."

Perhaps Daebaudjimod knew too much; but envy was more likely the root of some of the enmity that some people harboured for the story-teller.

Among those who did not like Daebaudjimod, were Mudjeekawis and Papeekawis. First, Daebaudjimod became a part of every festival; his story telling sometimes exceeded singing and dancing. Besides Mudjeekawis and Papeekawis, were somewhat self-righteous. The result was that whenever Daebaudjimod told of matters that seemed fantastic, the brothers scoffed and challenged the story-teller to verify his statements. They even called him names saying, "Liar, Boaster."

During Nanabush's wedding reception, Daebaudjimod entertained the guests with stories. While most Anishnabeg enjoyed these stories and found them amusing Papeekawis scoffed and snickered.

When, therefore, Daebaudjimod told of sea so large that man could not cross it and that it was so salty as to be undrinkable and when he told of men with white skins and beards, Papeekawiss, unable to match Daebaudjimod in story-telling challenged him to a game of plum stones after he had beaten all the other Anishnabeg at the game.

Daebaudjimod was unable to refuse Papeekawis' challenge in which Papeekawis wagered all his previous winnings on one toss. He said to Daebaudjimod, "All my winnings for your nephew. If I win, I will retain your nephew as my mizhiniwae, my messenger".

With one toss of the plum stones, Papeekawis won Daebaudjimod's nephew as his messenger.

Nevertheless, Daebaudjimod was able to teach the Anishnabeg how to make snow-shoes, canoes, cradle-boards, the bow and arrow, the quality of animal beings.

It was Daebaudjimod who taught orators persuasion, story-tellers imagination; singers poetry; speakers fluency; liars exaggeration.

NANABUSH

Nanabush was a paradox. On the one hand, he was a supernatural being possessing supernatural powers; on the other hand, he was the son of a mortal woman subject to the need to learn. He was sent to the world to teach the Anishnabeg, to help the weak, and to heal the sick. He could be human, but in nature and essence was a spirit.

Yet he was not a god. Though he had vast powers he was not considered the equal of Kitche Manitou. Rather Nanabush was a messenger of Kitche Manitou; an intermediary on earth between different species of beings; and, an advocate for the Anishnabeg.

To fulfil his purpose Nanabush had powers of transformation. At will and need, he could become a corporeal being of any species such as a willow tree, a beaver, a stump, or even a cloud.

Great and astonishing as was the power of self transformation, it had limitations. For Nanabush, in assuming another form, had to suffer the nature and the limitations of that form. For example, if he assumed the form of a snake, he had to be a snake with all the limitations of the snake, but having such powers and virtues possessed by snakes.

Nanabush was essentially an incorporeal being, even when he assumed a physical form. Though transformation seemed complete in a physical mode, it was never complete in the incorporeal sense. It was never perfect.

It was this aspect that made Nanabush a human, most unlike an incorporeal being. It was the human ideals of courage, generosity, resourcefulness, kindness that made him lovable; as it was human limitations of ineptitude, indecisiveness, inconstancy, cunning that made him a figure of fun.

As a youngster, Nanabush didn't know his powers or himself. When he realized that unlike most other youngsters he had no parents, he asked his grandmother about his origin. When he eventually learned that he had parents and of the alleged fate of his mother, he longed to know love. Feeling deprived of love and in a mood and spirit of vengeance, Nanabush set out to avenge his mother's death.

Nanabush was like any other young boy. He needed to learn and it was his grandmother who taught him the ways of the world, while Daebaudjimod showed him and gave him practical wisdom.

Like other boys, Nanabush had to fast and quest for vision. Just as other boys, he failed initially. In fact, in one of the first vigils, Nanabush yielded to hunger and thirst, so that instead of fasting and keeping vigil, Nanabush left the place of visions to hunt. At no time during his life was Nanabush more successful than on this occasion. He killed many deer and numerous birds, more than he needed. Hungry, desperately hungry, Nanabush ate. He gorged himself till he collapsed, unable to move, into a deep sleep.

It was in this state of stupor that his grandmother found him when she later came for him.

Eventually Nanabush received his vision. It was a vision of poverty that he would bring upon himself for helping others.

On his return from the west and after fighting his father, Nanabush embarked upon a career of assisting the Anishnabeg. He destroyed the two-headed serpents, released the Red Swan and made life safe for the Anishnabeg.

But Nanabush aided all beings, not only the Anishnabeg. He always came to the assistance of the oppressed and the weak. In turn, he aided the old men, the old women, the children, the helpless roses, the oppressed beaver, the poor porcupines.

160

Nanabush failed, yet he succeeded. He was a spirit; yet he was more human. Of all the incorporeal beings, Nanabush was best loved, but least understood.

THE FOUR GUARDIANS

Bebon was the spirit of winter, a being of vast power who usually exhausted himself by the very force of his intensity and endurance.

His abode was somewhere in the far north. And after the initial battle with Zeegwun, he was allowed to exercise his power alternately with Zeegwun for dominion over the land.

Bebon had control of the cold. With it, he caused sickness; he could make the leaves, fruits, berries wither; he could cover the earth with whiteness and the lakes and rivers with ice and make the fishes go deep into the lakes. Bebon was powerful.

While he did not cow every creature with his power, he tried to instil fear in everyone. But there were some who not only ignored him, but actually, taunted him. Such a one was Shingibis, the diver who did not change his habits or manner of living.

While most creatures had forsaken the land in winter, or cowered in cedar groves or trembled with chills, the diver seemed to enjoy winter as much as he did summer. He sang and looked cheerful during the coldest days and in the darkest blizzards. Such conditions only encouraged the diver to work harder, sing more cheerfully, and build a warmer fire. Other times he flew around, or skidded across the ice in play.

To Bebon, such conduct on the part of diver was open defiance and gesture of insult. For this, Bebon plotted to assassinate diver, or at least extract homage and respect from him. Bebon sent blizzard after blizzard; he sent snow-falls of every variety; he sent intense cold that cracked the rocks and the trees.

The diver only worked harder; he coughed more frequently, he sang more gaily. It seemed that the more force Bebon exerted, the more diver enjoyed the conditions, the more imaginative and resourceful he was.

At last Bebon gave up! He had exhausted his power and wasted his fury trying to overcome little diver. Finally weak, he withdrew in anger and humiliation to his domain in the north.

But Bebon was engaged in a more permanent contest, with Zeegwun, his mortal enemy. He was too busy during the peak of his power to overwhelm small enemies or imagined enemies because he had to concentrate on his struggle with Zeegwun.

By the time Zeegwun returned, refreshed, Bebon was dissipated and weak and too exhausted to resist Zeegwun.

ZEEGWUN

Zeegwun's abode was somewhere in the south, the land of Zhawanong, a place of perpetual heat and summer and flowers and song. Zeegwun is often pictured as a young man rather meek and docile, somewhat indolent and shy.

His was a never-ending struggle with Bebon, the old warrior. Unlike Bebon who brought destruction, hardship, and decay, Zeegwun brought life and growth.

The birds always heralded the arrival of Zeegwun. First, the crow; then not long afterward, the blue-bird arrived as messenger from the far south. Just a little later the trees began to shed their vital liquids as sap. When this occurred, the Anishnabeg knew that Zeegwun had arrived.

When Zeegwun came, all things came to life. The trees began to bud; little plants emerged through the soils; purple flowers opened to the sun, animals who had been sleeping, awakened; the young were born.

Bebon must retreat as he grows weaker. Life takes his place; death must yield to life, however, reluctantly.

Like Bebon, Zeegwun has vast powers of life-giving and regeneration, becoming and changing; and like Bebon, Zeegwun has limitations.

When he should be bold, direct, forthright, and forceful, Zeegwun is circumspect and somewhat timid and bashful. This his undoing.

Having defeated Bebon, perhaps Zeegwun might have laboured to keep Bebon in exile. But confident that his victory was final and that Bebon would not revive or come back Zeegwun forgot about his enemy. In fact, Zeegwun engaged in pursuits that had nothing to do with his nature and purpose. He fell in love.

One time, Zeegwun fell in love with a maiden in yellow hair. By the time he had collected his courage to tell her of his love and to ask her to be his wife, she died. On another occasion, he fell in love with a young maiden whose eyes were as lustrous as polished flint. He waited too long. She fell in love with someone else. Bitterly, he decided not to love again.

But the next summer, he returned to the country and fell in love once more. He was unable to control love. But as he was about to marry the young lady, Bebon arrived to challenge him for the young lady's affections. This was how the long feuding began between Bebon and Zeegwun, between life and death, regeneration and disintegration. These are the spirits who represent physical time in terms of the seasons.

WAUBUN

Waubun, a young medicine man under the tutelage of Ningo-bianong, also superintended the east and youth. Initially, as understudy to the elder medicine man, Waubun was quite happy. But as he grew older and gained more knowledge, he wanted to conduct his own healing. He felt that he knew as much as Ningobianong and challenged him to a contest of powers. Though his powers were great, they were all negated by Ningobianong. It was then that the conflict between youth and age, between knowledge and wisdom began with the fight between the medicine men. Waubun represented only the first portion of man's time, Ningobianong the other.

NINGOBIANONG

Ningobianong was a medicine man fully accredited, representing old age and wisdom, whose realm was the west. Besides healing he tried to teach the need for moderation, patience, fortitude. Until he had imparted these qualities to the young man, Waubun, who was headstrong, Ningobianong could not allow the young man to conduct the affairs of healing and prolonging life.

It was Ningobianong's refusal to release Waubun from his obligation to learn more that led to the estrangement between them. For Waubun, Ningobianong's refusal was tantamount to bondage; to Ningobianong, Waubun's desire for independence was a betrayal of a trust.

Ningobianong represented a force in life contrary to that of Waubun. Their conflict images the lasting conflict within human experience.

PAUGUK (Flying Skeleton)

Two sons told their parents that they were going down to the lake to paddle around. Later that day a violent storm erupted and continued well on into the night. When the boys did not return, the parents were alarmed.

That night as the parents were waiting for the storm to subside they heard thin wails of anguish coming from the shores. Thoroughly frightened, but hopeful the parents rushed down to the rocky shores.

The waves were crashing against the rocks, the wind was howling. But someone was shrieking in pain and terror above the thundering waves. Mother and Father ran to and fro calling out for their sons.

"Here," came the answer. But the answer was not the voice of either son. And in the dark it was hard to see. The parents ran to the place where the voice was coming from.

"Here," came the shrieking voice, piercing the night and the courage of the parents. They looked. And to their horror, they saw a skeleton wedged in the rocks struggling to get out beckoning its fleshless arms to them and whining in this whistling-like voice, "Help me."

The man and his wife froze in terror,

"Help me," pleaded the skeleton,

The husband and wife were unable to reply,

"Help me," implored the skeleton.

"I dare not," rasped the man, "A living being must not, cannot touch the dead. It is not natural that the dead return to the life of the living or that the dead ask help from those not yet dead," continued the man.

"Help me, Have pity on me. I cannot harm nor would I harm you, were I able. Set me free from these rocks."

"Who are you," asked the man screwing up more courage.

The skeleton shrieked, "I am Pauguk. My destiny is ever to wail my fault and to spend eternity not in the Land of Souls, but in the skies to be blown about by the winds, to be either chilled by the cold or scorched by the sun."

"Why must you live out eternity in this way?" inquired the man.

Pauguk told his story. "I had a brother whose girl friend I coveted.

Though she was promised to him from birth and even though she loved my brother, I nevertheless wanted her for my own. I, therefore, sought ways of alienating them and then of winning her affection. It seemed that the only way of gaining the young woman was by killing my brother."

"I planned and worked out a number of accidents. Somehow my brother escaped and managed to avoid these traps. I, at last, went to a medicine man for help. On the pretext that I wanted a solution for a certain animal, I induced the medicine man to prepare a medicine for me.

"At home, I invited my brother to go fishing with me the following day. We fished all day spearing numerous whitefish. When we stopped for a meal I brewed a tea into which I poured the mixture and gave it to my brother. Without suspecting anything he drank the mixture, only to collapse and die a few moments later.

"To my astonishment, my brother's body diminished in size and became a pebble. I took the stone and paddling far out on the lake, I threw my brother's body in the waters. The instant the small corpse sank, the water turned murky.

"On my return home, even before I could explain my brother's absence I was asked by everyone, family and stranger alike, 'Where is your brother?' It was as if people knew. Thereafter, people avoided me. I was without a friend as an exile. I tried moving to new and different villages, but there was no acceptance.

"When I died, I was rejected even by those in the Land of Peace. Unable to find regeneration in the living world, I found myself in the world not on earth nor in the Land of Peace. This is the penalty for those who have done injury through malice to their fellow human beings."

Pauguk whined again, "Set me free."

The man refused, "No, the living must not touch the dead."

Pauguk fairly whistled and rattled, "If you can touch death, you live; to be without sympathy even for the dead is worse. No harm will befall you."

The man shook and was repelled but he removed the bones from the rock. When all the bones were released, the skeleton ascended whistling, wailing, and rattling into the skies.

Next day, after the storm had subsided, the two sons of the man and woman returned home. They told their parents that when the storm arose, they took refuge on an island some distance from the mainland.

WEENDIGO

There was a man named Weendigo, who lived on the north shores of Lake Nipissing.

For many years he and his family lived happily and fully on the plentiful game and fish that abounded in the country and the lake.

But conditions changed. Animals became scarce and fish rare. For all his skill, Weendigo's family began to starve. So desperate was he that at last he and his family began to eat the inner bark of trees and to make soup from barks.

Weendigo went days from home toward Temagami and south as far as Madawaska and as far west as Georgian Bay, but such long journeys were pointless. He might get game but how was he going to get it back.

He prayed to Kitche Manitou, but his own circumstances did not improve. He went for help to a Waubeno from whom Weendigo obtained a potion for hunting success. Weendigo was to take one small portion each day. According to the prescription, the medicine would soon take effect. That night Weendigo took a pinch and mixed it in the form of a tea, which he drank just before going to bed.

Very early the next day, he woke up while it was still dark. Convinced that there was no point in remaining in bed, Weendigo quietly rose and left the house. Outside, he was astonished at the length of his strides and the speed with which he covered the ground. In no time he had gone from Nippissing to Temagami to Temiskaming where he found a village of people standing around a great fire. Emerging from the woods and for fun, he gave three war cries. At the frightening call, the people and the children fell into a faint and changed into beavers.

Without thinking too much about the transformation of people into beavers, Weendigo considered the circumstance as a matter of good fortune and timely. He was hungry and famine did not allow him the luxury of questioning good fortune. Weendigo picked up the beaver, fifteen in all and skinned them. Then on the fire that had been prepared by the people of the village, Weendigo roasted all the beaver. When they were done, he sat down to eat.

He didn't eat; Weendigo stuffed himself. In fact, he ate all fifteen beavers. Nor did it occur to Weendigo to question his enormous appetite. He didn't stop to wonder how he could eat more than one beaver; he didn't even stop to consider whether he should carry the beaver home to his family. He thought only of himself. What was even more astonishing than the transformation and his appetite was his increase. For the more Weendigo ate, the greater he grew in size and the greater was his hunger. Instead of alleviating his hunger, Weendigo, by his very act of eating, actually fostered more and greater hunger.

Weendigo, larger and hungrier, left Temiskaming and proceeded north. It seemed that the further north he went, the more game there was. Weendigo's hunger superseded everything else, even his family and village. His need had first to be served and satisfied. In James Bay, Weendigo ate and ate, killed and killed.

In the meanwhile, Megis (shell) had returned from a long journey to his home around Temiskaming to find his village devastated and his people vanished.

Despondent, Megis went to a medicine man for guidance and help. As required by the medicine man, Megis went into vigil where in dream, he saw the fate of his people and village. His patron and tutelary, the bear, appeared to him and disclosed a solution to render him powerful enough to challenge Weendigo.

166

Megis, next day, made the medicine. After he took the medicine, Megis began to grow. When he had attained a very great height, Megis went in search of Weendigo. By following the tracks of Weendigo, Megis found it easy to locate Weendigo on the shores of James Bay.

Without waiting, Megis attacked Weendigo; and in a short while, slew Weendigo, badly weakened from hunger.

With Weendigo's death, his victims revived, Weendigo himself, though dead, continued to live on as an incorporeal being, the spirit of excess. As the spirit of excess, Weendigo could captivate or enslave anyone too preoccupied with sleep or work or play or drink or any pursuit or occupation. Children and the young were often warned, "Don't play too much, Weendigo will get you."

Though Weendigo was fearsome and visited punishment upon those committing excesses, he nevertheless conferred rewards upon the moderate. He was excess who encouraged moderation.

MAEMAEGAWAESUK

Kitche Manitou wrought the mountains, the cliffs, precipices, and escarpments. Thinking that perhaps the massive rocks were too imposing and dark and grey and dreary, Kitche Manitou fashioned small stones, the size of plum pits and of brilliant hues of white, crimson, green, blue, yellow, amber, azure. He hurled these brilliant pebbles against the mountains and rocky sides of the earth. Immediately, the rocks and mountains began to sparkle. The Anishnabeg found the shimmering rocks and mountains more beautiful than anything else, and ceased admiring other beautiful things.

When Nanabush came to live among the Anishnabeg, he found the people inordinately fond of rocky and mountainous places, so much so that they neglected the meadows and the forests. Nanabush complained to Kitche Manitou saying, "The Anishnabeg are so fond of the many coloured mountains that they have forsaken other forms of beauty. Besides, while only grown up men and women may enjoy these beauties, there is very little for infants and the very young. Can you not remove the gemstones from the mountains and give them to children. The mountains need not lose their majesty or their character."

Kitche Manitou agreed that there was little in the physical world to bring joy and happiness to children. He, therefore, permitted Nanabush to "Do what needs to be done."

Nanabush, after some thought, collected all the coloured

pebbles and threw them to the winds. The stones immediately changed into butterflies (Maemaegawaesuk) of soft and many colours, fluttering and dancing in the wind. They made the eyes of children twinkle. They became the spirit of children's play. On death, the butterflies changed again into beings who inhabited glades and glens seeking children to play with.

PAWEESUK

Inhabiting the sandy shores of lakes were the Paweesuk (pukwadjiinineesuk) who emerged from their sanctuaries on moonlit nights to dance in the shadows.

They danced on the beaches to warn people of the fearful Nebaunabe (mermaid) who lured people into the lakes. The Paweesuk feared Nebaunabe and especially drowning. It was to prevent drowning which to them was the most repugnant form of death that they warned people of the waters by making the dance and the shadows more enticing and alluring at night.

The Paweesuk were small and frail, easily frightened and injured. More than water and drowning, the Paweesuk dreaded and despised Kawaesind, The Feared. They were weak, he was strong. They were considerate, he was heartless. They were humble; he was overbearing. His strength and weakness were in his head both at the same time.

Paweesuk learned that Kawaesind's physical weakness resided in his skull; that though he was immune to many things, he was subject to harm by seed-cones. The Paweesuk decided to do in Kawaesind, before he overpowered them. They, therefore, waited in ambush; watched him at every turn. Their opportunity came when one of the scouts reported that Kawaesind was fishing in the middle of Toquaminaing river. As soon as this bit of intelligence was received, the Paweesuk assembled downstream, armed with seed-cones, and concealed in the tree tops and limbs that overhung the river.

When Kawaesind returned the Paweesuk attacked him as he paddled underneath the overhanging trees. Mortally wounded and trying to protect himself, Kawaesind upset his canoe. Too badly injured, Kawaesind drowned.

Safe, the Paweesuk danced the dance of triumph that night.

MISSABIKONG (Little Man of Iron)

Missabikong or Missabikum imaged the character and nature of rock, solid, abiding, strong. He inhabited grottoes and unique formations, deep chasms wherever there was a place suitable for visions. Seldom seen, Missabikong is very obscure.

NAWNEEDIS (Patron of Health)

The sick were treated not only with herbs and medicines for their physical well being; in the name and through the name of Nawneedis, the inner well being of a person was fostered and sought. Nawneedis was the patron of well being.

NEBAUNAUBE OR NEBAUNAUBAEQUAE

During a vicious storm two young men who had been fishing took refuge on the shores of a bay. They were lying comfortably underneath a lean-to that they had constructed of cedar some distance from the beach, and watching a fire when they heard above the crash of the waves, the plaintive voice of a woman coming from the shore.

Mizaun (Burr), according to the story, over the warnings of his companion not to heed the call rushed down to the beach to rescue whoever was in distress. Not finding anyone on the beach, but still hearing the voice some distance out in the lake, Mizaun dashed into the waters.

When he reached the drowning woman, Mizaun was unable to bring her back to the shore. He was, as he later recounted, pulled under.

When he regained consciousness, he was among Fish-beings who were part human and part fish. What was even more remarkable was that they could transform themselves into beings completely of the nature and form of water beings or of human beings.

From the fish or water-beings, he learned that he had come through four levels of life or death before arriving in the land of the Water Beings.

Alarmed, Mizaun declared that he would return to his people in the Land of the Living. The spokesman for the water-beings shook his head, not sadly, but assuredly, telling Mizaun that he would never go back from whence he had come. Moreover, the spokesman told Mizaun that he was to marry the woman who had brought him there, that he would father many children, he would not wish to return to the people of his own land, and that Mizaun would attempt to bring many of his own people to the Land of the Water Beings.

Mizaun was confounded, not only by this intelligence but by his apparent lack of sadness.

As predicted by the spokesman, Mizaun married the woman who had pulled him under the waves. Together they had many children. Mizaun was happy and content in his new home and with his new brothers and sisters, the water-beings. Still he longed to see his own people, not from sorrow, but from curiosity.

He therefore asked his wife if he could go back to visit the people and especially his parents. Permission was granted to Mizaun and his children to visit the Land of the Living on the understanding that it might cause some sorrow. Still Mizaun resolved to go.

On his return to the Land of the Living, Mizaun found himself on the beach that he had left, the storm still raging and his companion calling out to him over the waters. Mizaun was dumbfounded. How could this be? How could he have gone, married, and fathered children while the same storm still disturbed the lake, while his companion shouted for him through the gale? At most a few minutes had passed on the upper earth. Mizaun's descent was measured by another time.

"Needjee, maumpee! (Friend, here!)" Mizaun yelled out above the thundering waves and whistling wind, as he swam to the shore.

Numae (Sturgeon) watched his friend emerge from the waves with fear and consternation.

He managed to stutter, "You are just a form, a shape! Nebaunaubaequae (Nebauh — sleep; naube — being; quae — woman) has seized you! How many times I warned you that this would happen! What shall I tell your parents?"

Mizaun placed a hand on his friend's shoulder. "Don't feel sorry for me, and don't blame yourself. I am perfectly happy with my new life. I shall go to my parents myself."

Mizaun left Numae on the beach and appeared to his parents in their dreams, recounting the events and adventures of the night which seemed years ago to him, but was last night to them.

His mother wept; his father lamented, "We warned you of Nebaunaubaequae so many times. You didn't listen. Now she has taken hold of you, my son, and we will never see you again." He too wept.

Mizaun did his best to console his parents with accounts of his happiness among the water-beings, promising to come to visit them from time to time, but his parents were inconsolable. Mizaun offered to take them with him into the Land of the water-beings, where his children and he, himself lived in happiness. No matter what he said, they refused with a shudder.

Mizaun returned to his adoptive people, the water-beings, saddened but content at last that he would never live in the upper world again.

MISHEEKAEHN OR MAKINAK — The Turtle

Since he served mankind by offering his back as a haven of rest to Nokomis, and lending his back for the re-creation of the world, the turtle has a special place in the realm of the natural and the supernatural. As a token of appreciation, Nokomis conferred upon the turtle unique powers transcending his physical and spatial scope and being, enabling him to transgress time periods from present to future or to the past and back again; and to transform his being from its physical to an incorporeal nature. As such the turtle became not only a symbol but the actual medium of communication between beings of this world and time and beings of another world and dimension of time. The turtle continues to serve medicine men (Jeesekeewininiwuk) as patron.

CPSIA information can be obtained
at www.ICGtesting.com
Printed in the USA
LVHW012357110721
692329LV00003BA/3